Policy Arrogance or Innocent Bias

Resetting Citizenship and Multiculturalism

Andrew Griffith

Published by Anar Press

Library and Archives Canada Cataloguing in Publication

Griffith, Andrew, author
Policy arrogance or innocent bias? : resetting citizenship and multiculturalism / Andrew Griffith.

Issued in print and electronic formats.
ISBN 978-0-9880640-4-1 (pbk.).--ISBN 978-0-9880640-7-2 (kobo).--
ISBN 978-0-9880640-6-5 (kindle).--ISBN 978-0-9880640-5-8 (iTunes)

1. Citizenship--Canada. 2. Multiculturalism--Canada. I. Title.

JL187.G75 2013   323.60971   C2013-907098-2
C2013-905302-6

To Nazanine, Alex and Roxanne for their ongoing encouragement, support and love.

Preface

Late one Friday afternoon in August 2007, I received a call from Jason Kenney, then Secretary of State for Multiculturalism. It was my first day on the job. Minister Kenney asked why I had not approved his office's proposed language in a press release. I blurted out, "But Minister, it doesn't sound Ministerial …"

After a weekend of wondering whether I would still have my position as Director General for Multiculturalism, I survived, and went on to work with him and his staff for close to four years, first at Canadian Heritage and then at Citizenship and Immigration Canada (CIC), following the transfer of the multicultural program to CIC in October 2008 after Kenney's appointment as Minister of Citizenship, Immigration and Multiculturalism.

During this period, citizenship (added to my responsibilities at CIC) and multiculturalism policies and programs were fundamentally reset, in line with the government's emphasis on more meaningful citizenship and more integrative multiculturalism.

This book is about my learning to become more modest about the degree of expertise and knowledge that my team and I had with respect to citizenship and multiculturalism, forced by the radically different perspective that the Harper government and Minister Kenney brought to these inherently complex social policy issues. It is also the story of how officials balanced the public service challenge function role of "fearless advice" with the need to serve the government of the day through "loyal implementation." Given the sharp nature of the policy reset, and the entrenched views of many public servants, this book aims to provide a small case study of how public servants adjusted to the new reality — one in which their expertise was fundamentally challenged, discounted, and at times ignored.

In many cases, officials had to work through the Kübler-Ross stages of grief and loss — denial, anger, bargaining, depression, and acceptance — in dealing with the traumatic challenge to their role, as well as to the long-standing consensus between previous Liberal and Conservative parties on citizenship and multiculturalism issues.

I also aim to address, in part, the paucity of literature by Canadian policy makers on the interface between the political and bureaucratic levels. While much has been written by academics on citizenship and multiculturalism policies themselves, and there is an equally large body of academic work on public policy development, relatively few "in the trenches" accounts exist, and this book aims to fill partially this gap. I do not attempt to provide a fully objective and comprehensive account. Others, at both the political and official levels, may have different interpretations. However, I hope to enrich public policy understanding through sharing what was an intense and interesting time of policy change and political-bureaucratic interface challenges.

Table of Contents

POLICY ARROGANCE OR INNOCENT BIAS

Context

Canada's citizenship and multiculturalism policies reflect Canada's history, identity and values as they have evolved and continue to evolve. Unique among immigration-based countries, Canada is made up of a mix of aboriginal peoples, French, British, and successive waves of other communities, which has allowed Canada to develop more of a culture of accommodation and acceptance of diversity from its inception.[1] The development of global and national human rights frameworks and legislation further strengthened this trend, as did the growing civic participation of both established and newer immigrant populations, making Canadian political parties responsive to and reflective of increased diversity.

While aspects of globalization, including cheap travel, virtually free international communications, and the development of specialty media to serve individual ethnic communities has provided alternatives to integration, on the whole most large scale surveys demonstrate comparable behaviour between Canadian and foreign-born residents.

The overall result, while not perfect, has been a generally welcoming society, one not fraught with many of the backlashes in other countries. In Canada, political and policy debates tend to revolve around the details of policies and programs, rather than question the fundamentals of Canada's model of immigration and citizenship.[2]

Traditional Canadian diversity — aboriginal, French, English, other European — became considerably broader since immigration restrictions on non-European immigration were lifted in the 1960s, as seen in the graph below:[3]

---

[1] See Will Kymlicka, *Canadian Multiculturalism in Historical and Comparative Perspective: Is Canada Unique?* In Constitutional Forum, Vol 13, No 1 & 2 (2003), among his other writings.

[2] There are of course numerous critics of these policies (e.g., Gilles Paquet, Martin Collacott, Salim Mansour, Neil Bissoondath). A good survey of just how different Canada is from other countries in its acceptance of immigration and multiculturalism can be found in Irene Bloemraad's Understanding "Canadian Exceptionalism" in Immigration and Pluralism Policy, Migration Policy Institute, July 2012.

[3] Data from Canadian Diversity 1871 - 2017, Annual Report on the Operation of the Canadian Multiculturalism Act 2010-2011.

Chart 1: Evolution of Canadian Diversity: 1867 — 2017

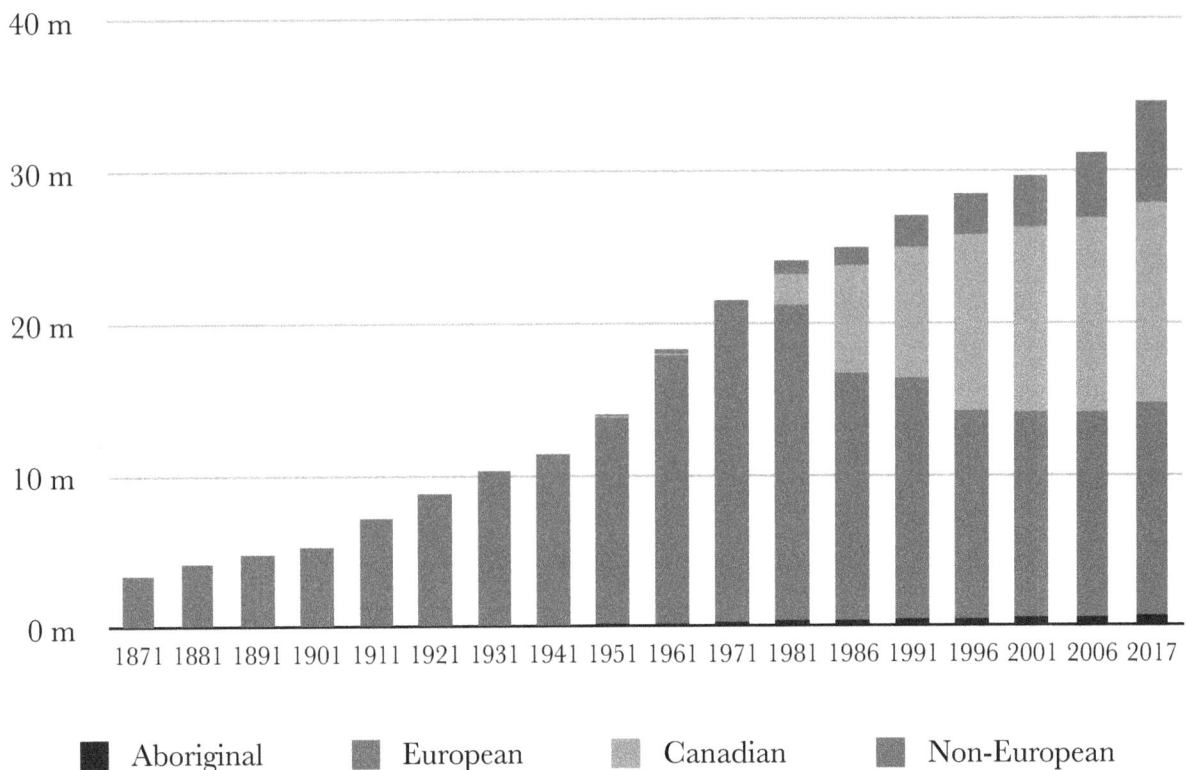

Like many government policies, citizenship and multiculturalism reflected a balance of apparently opposing objectives. For citizenship, the balance was between meaningfulness, or the integrity and depth of the citizenship process, and facilitation, or the encouragement of becoming citizens as part of the integration process. Alternatively stated, attaining citizenship could either reflect being integrated, or it could be an important way station to further integration. For multiculturalism, the balance was between integration, or becoming more like the Canadian mainstream, and accommodation, or the mainstream becoming more accepting of the diversity of habits and cultures of ethnic communities.

While Canadian citizenship and multiculturalism has always been open to political interpretation, both Conservative and Liberal governments emphasized the facilitation of citizenship and accommodation of diversity as a means to promote integration within the context of Canadian laws and values.

Canadian multiculturalism policy, along with citizenship, has evolved over the years. While the overall trend of citizenship policy tended towards facilitation, multiculturalism was slowly evolving in the other direction as Canada's diversity became increasingly mainstream, and a number of long-term integration issues became apparent.

For citizenship, this trend can be seen in the following changes in the policy over past years of Liberal and Conservative government:

- Changes to *The Citizenship Act* in 1977 that:

  - Eliminated practices that discriminated on the basis of race or ethnic origin (e.g., related to the special treatment of British nationals in the citizenship process);

  - Removed discrimination on passing down citizenship based upon gender or marital status;

  - Permitted dual citizenship; and,

  - Lowered the residency requirement from five years to three years.

- Introduction in the 1990s of a citizenship test and study guide, *A Look at Canada*, driven as much by administrative needs to simplify meeting the requirements of the *Act* as by substantive interest in improving knowledge about Canada;

- Lowering of the exemption from the citizenship test from 60 to 55 in 2005; and,

- Arguably, allowing foreign-born adopted children to become Canadian citizens without passing through permanent residency requirements, and addressing many of the issues related to "Lost Canadians," or previous discrimination on the basis of marital status and gender in passing on Canadian citizenship in 2009.[4]

For multiculturalism, the following table summarizes how the program has evolved over the years from ethnicity-focused multiculturalism ("celebrating our differences") to inclusive citizenship and integration:[5]

---

[4] The counterpart was the tightening of passing on citizenship across generations through the imposition of the first generation limit.

[5] Fleras, A. & Jean Kunz, *Media and Minorities: representing diversity in a Multicultural Canada* (Toronto: Thompson Education Publishing, 2001), updated with the "harmony/jazz" metaphor in *From Mosaic to Harmony: Multicultural Canada in the 21st Century: Results of Regional Roundtables*, (Policy Research Institute, 2007). This applies more to English Canada than Quebec; while both are in the phase of "integrative multiculturalism," Quebec is more inspired by France's Cartesian model, with more clearly defined frameworks, than the more improvisational approach of "dialogue/mutual understanding" and 'harmony/jazz' (Bouchard-Taylor Commission excepted).

POLICY ARROGANCE OR INNOCENT BIAS

Table 1: Multiculturalism Program Evolution

	Ethnicity Multi (1970s)	Equity Multi (1980s)	Civic Multi (1990s)	Integrative Multi (2000s)
Focus	Celebrating differences	Managing diversity	Constructive engagement	Inclusive citizenship
Reference Point	Culture	Structure	Society building	Canadian identity
Mandate	Ethnicity	Race relations	Citizenship	Integration
Magnitude	Individual adjustment	Accommodation	Participation	Rights and Responsibilities
Problem Source	Prejudice	Systemic discrimination	Exclusion	Unequal access, "clash" of cultures
Solution	Cultural sensitivity	Employment equity	Inclusiveness	Dialogue/Mutual understanding
Key Metaphor	"Mosaic"	"Level playing field"	"Belonging"	"Harmony/Jazz"

As in so many other areas, the dynamics in Quebec were different, with a more Cartesian approach to integration issues, existentialist in nature and French in inspiration, rather than the more fluid and *ad hoc* approach characteristic of the rest of Canada (the "harmony/jazz" approach).

The arrival of the new Conservative government in 2006, with the Reform skepticism of many of these policies, marked a change towards a more "muscular" and explicit focus on meaningfulness and integration. While much of the initial Reform Party platforms focused on immigration (economic focus, tightening up of the refugee system, being more attuned to public concerns), nothing was said about citizenship. However, considerable emphasis was put on changing the multiculturalism program in the 1996-97 Blue Book:

Multiculturalism

A. The Reform Party stands for the acceptance and integration of immigrants to Canada into the mainstream of Canadian life. The Reform Party would focus Federal Government activities on enhancing the citizenship of all Canadians regardless of race, language or culture.

B. The Reform Party of Canada opposes the current concept of multiculturalism and hyphenated Canadianism pursued by the Government of Canada. We would end funding of the multicultural program and support the abolition of the Department of Multiculturalism.

C. The Reform Party supports and shall uphold the principle that
   individuals or groups are free to preserve their cultural heritage using
   their own resources.[6]

However, the new Conservative party platforms were largely silent on these aims. Even with one of the leading thinkers of the Reform Party at 24 Sussex, elements of continuity were present. The new government was committed to recognizing historical immigration and wartime restrictions for a number of communities, building on the Mulroney government's recognition of Japanese Canadian internment, and driven in part by electoral considerations. Similarly, the government understood demographics, carrying out extensive outreach to a large number of ethnocultural communities, to build links necessary to electoral success.[7]

But a shift was clear. Rather than citizenship being "easy," as a stepping stone towards integration, more effort would be required, in terms of knowledge and language, to become a citizen, and the abuse of residency requirements would be countered by increased emphasis on integrity and enforcement. The evacuation of Lebanese-Canadians during the Israel-Lebanon conflict in 2006, early on in the government's tenure, and the large number of Canadian citizens with minimal connection to Canada, underlined the issues with current citizenship policy.[8]

Rather than multiculturalism being defined as relations between the mainstream (code for "white" Canadians) and other ethnicities, the focus was broadened to include relations between and among all communities, along with the downplaying of the traditional emphasis on racism and discrimination issues, and the highlighting of antisemitism.

The following table captures the main government initiatives that reflected these shifts in policy:

---

[6] p. 33, Reform Party Blue Book, 1996-97; Conservative Party platforms in 2004 and 2006 were silent.

[7] One of the ironies was the government was using Statistics Canada ethnic diversity and multiculturalism data just as it was announcing the end of the mandatory long-form census.

[8] See Canadians of convenience, Macleans, 20 November 2006, among numerous other articles.

Table 2: Citizenship and Multiculturalism Policy Shifts

Meaningful Citizenship	Integrative Multiculturalism
• Granting citizenship to children adopted abroad (C-14) • Granting citizenship to "Lost Canadians" and applying a first-generation limit (C-37) to transmission of citizenship rights • The new *Discover Canada* citizenship guide and more rigorous knowledge test • Tighter language requirements • Revocation, physical residency, and controls on consultants	• New program objectives focused on integration • Links to civic values and memory • New approach to racism and discrimination with focus on particular communities (e.g., antisemitism) • Inclusion of faith-related issues • Similarities between *interculturalisme* (Quebec) and multiculturalism (Canada-wide)

In parallel, widespread Conservative suspicion and distrust of the Charter, employment equity, and human rights legislation and bodies, in reaction to what was perceived as some of the excesses of some of the human rights claims and decisions, reinforced this shift.[9]

These changes did not take place in isolation from other immigration-related policy changes. The transfer of the multiculturalism program to CIC reflected the intent to have coherence between the various policy instruments: immigration, integration (settlement), citizenship and multiculturalism. CIC had to adjust its CIC "continuum" among these policy instruments, in a broader manner than the linear, sequential processing mindset of CIC (selecting immigrants first, providing language instruction, and then make them citizens) to account for multiculturalism, which addressed long-term integration issues and thus included all Canadians, whether first generation or long-established, whether minority (e.g., Ukrainian Canadians, Black Canadians) or majority (traditional European groups).[10] The following graphic tries to capture this relationship, and how immigration, integration and citizenship policies reflect Canadian values and identity, including multiculturalism:

---

[9] See Tories take aim at employment equity, *The Globe and Mail*, 22 July 2010.

[10] One of the consequences of this linear thinking was the belief among some that immigrant selection could take into account the long-term integration challenges by factoring them into selection criteria. While valid when on the basis of language and other competencies, previous efforts to select immigrants on the basis of culture or origin were abandoned in the 1960s and have been repudiated through the Community Historical Recognition Program and Chinese Head Tax Program.

Chart 2: Situating Immigration, Integration and Citizenship within Broader Context

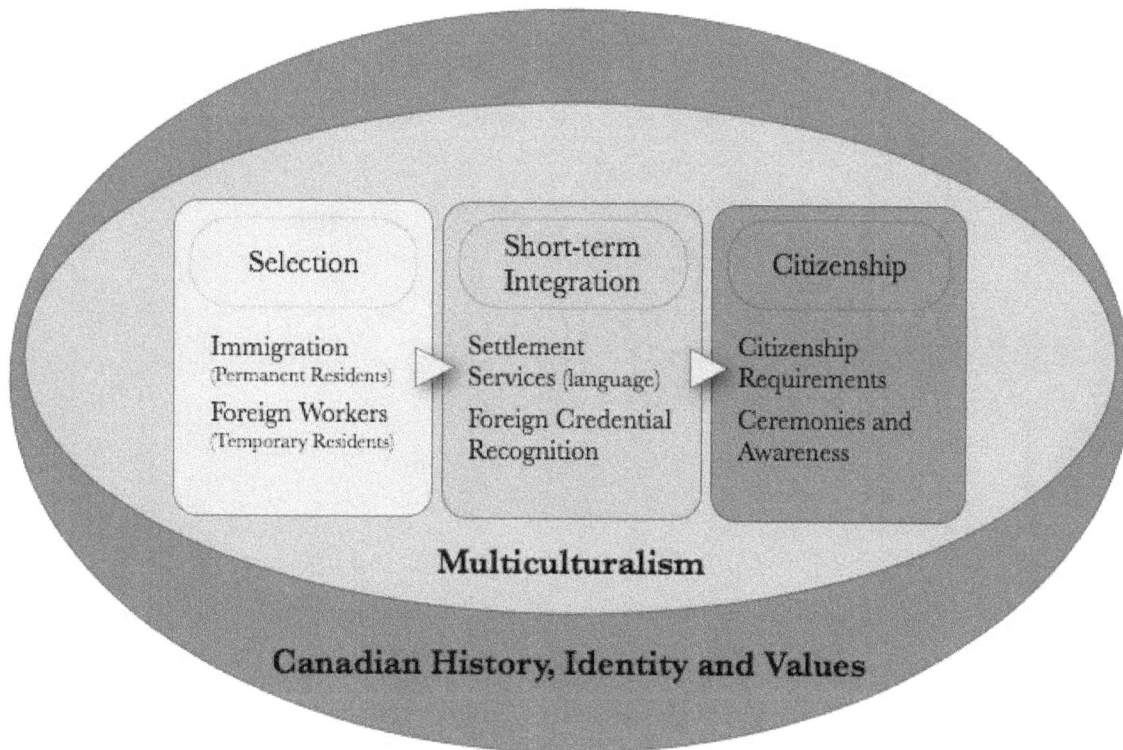

To complement these changes, the immigration program emphasized economic immigration more than family reunification and refugee protection, placed greater weight on official language competency, and encouraged more temporary foreign workers. The end results were a shift in the mix of immigrants in terms of source countries (Appendix C), categories and language (Appendix D).[11]

---

[11] Ratna Omidvar, among others, has argued that the cumulative effects of a number of immigration-related policies has weakened the connection between immigration, citizenship and belonging. See Temporary immigrants mean temporary loyalties, *The Globe and Mail*, 20 May 2013. The recent public controversy over the scale and role of foreign workers, and the government's efforts to apply more rigor to the program, are another manifestation of the changed policies. See Foreign worker program gets new rules, higher fees, *CBC*, 29 April 2013.

POLICY ARROGANCE OR INNOCENT BIAS

The government became enamored of the word "pluralism" rather than multiculturalism; the former becoming part of many a prime ministerial or ministerial speech.[12] Ultimately, of course, the reference to multiculturalism in the Charter imposed limits to change, and the focus became substantively on emphasizing the integration aspects of multiculturalism, not accommodation.[13]

---

[12] Some early examples include: "Pluralism is the principle that binds our diverse peoples together" (PM Harper's speech announcing Global Centre for Pluralism, 25 October 2006), "our model of pluralism and immigration" (Minister Kenney speech to the Annual Diplomatic Forum, December 17, 2008), "hard work of making a pluralistic society work and to create and maintain true unity in our country's great diversity" (Minister Kenney, launch of Discover Canada, 12 November 2009). But the government was somewhat schizophrenic on this point, introducing the Paul Yuzyk Award on Multiculturalism, which "commemorates the late Senator Yuzyk's pioneering legacy in establishing multiculturalism as one of the fundamental characteristics of Canadian heritage and identity" (Paul Yuzyk award, CIC website).

[13] Multiculturalism, pluralism, and interculturalism are all, to a certain extent, "plastic" words that can be interpreted and shaped. In the Canadian context, multiculturalism tends to have a broad, inclusive meaning, rather than just referring to ethnocultural communities. See Has multiculturalism hit a bump in the road?, *The Toronto Star*, 5 July 2013.

Chapter 1

Introduction

One of the tests of any parliamentary democracy is the professionalism, responsiveness, and loyalty of the public service in adjusting to the different priorities and perspectives of a new government. This book examines what happens when the public service is challenged in these aspects, from the perspective of someone who lived it in citizenship and multiculturalism policy from fall 2007 to spring 2011.

Public service professionalism and loyalty in this respect is formally defined by the *Values and Ethics Code for the Public Sector*, in the section on *Respect for Democracy*:

> Public servants shall uphold the Canadian parliamentary democracy and its institutions by:
>
> 1.1 Respecting the rule of law and carrying out their duties in accordance with legislation, policies and directives in a non-partisan and impartial manner.
>
> 1.2 Loyally carrying out the lawful decisions of their leaders and supporting ministers in their accountability to Parliament and Canadians.
>
> 1.3 Providing decision makers with all the information, analysis and advice they need, always striving to be open, candid and impartial.[14]

These behaviours were severely tested following the election of the Conservative government in 2006, and the appointment of Jason Kenney as Secretary of State for Multiculturalism in early 2007 (he subsequently became Minister for Citizenship, Immigration and Multiculturalism), given the break with the high degree of policy continuity between previous Liberal and Conservative governments on citizenship and multiculturalism policies.

As noted by Prime Minister Harper in 2008, one of the main challenges for an incoming government, especially one with limited governing experience, is learning how to manage the relationship between the political sphere and the bureaucratic one, and particularly when implementing a significantly different policy agenda:

> Probably the most difficult job, you know, practical difficult thing you have to learn as a prime minister and ministers, our ministers as well, is dealing with the federal bureaucracy. ... It's walking that fine line of, of being a positive leader of the federal public service, but at the same time pushing

---

[14] <u>Values and Ethics Code for the Public Sector</u>, Treasury Board website.

them and not becoming captive to them. ... I could write a book on that one.[15]

This "fine line" was further stressed as the government pushed its agenda of citizenship that was more meaningful and exacting, and multiculturalism that focused on integration over accommodation. Public servants had internalized the previous policy of continuity and consensus; the Minister's direction posed an almost existentialist challenge to the role and expertise of the public service, as he and his officials constantly — and fundamentally — challenged prevailing policies, programs, and perspectives. The emphasis was more on pushing than positive leadership, necessary given the entrenched "conventional wisdom" and inertia of the bureaucracy.[16]

The depth of the desired policy change challenged in turn the "mantra" of the relationship between the political and official levels. Whether referred to as "truth to power" or the preferable "fearless advice and loyal implementation," the respective roles had been generally understood. Public servants have the obligation to tell the political level directly what public service expertise and advice suggested, while Ministers have the obligation to listen and consider that advice.[17] Ministers have the "right to be wrong"; officials have the obligation to implement decisions, irrespective of their views. But as Donald Savoie, among others, has noted, the long-term trend has been towards a reduced policy role for the public service:

> It's not too much of an exaggeration to write that the policy advisory role of public servants in Anglo-American democracies has been turned on its head. Multiple sources of information and evidence-based policy advice no longer matter as they once did. Today, if policy-making in a post-positivism world is a matter of opinion, where 2 + 2 can equal 5, then Google searches, focus groups, public opinion surveys and a well-connected lobbyist can provide any policy answer that politicians wish to hear.[18]

---

[15] Quoted in Susan Delacourt, Tory government takes aim at bureaucracy, *The Toronto Star*, 17 January 2008

[16] This is not to excuse the numerous and well-documented examples of excesses by the Harper Government, but any major change of policy requires major pushing by the political level.

[17] "Truth to power" has the connotation that only public servants have the "truth," hence it is less used. The formal iteration in the Values and Ethics Code for the Public Service has undergone an evolution from "professional, candid and frank advice" (previous code) to the somewhat softer "open, candid and impartial" (current code), although the latter also makes reference to Ministers' responsibility to "supporting public servants' responsibility to provide professional and frank advice."

[18] Donald Savoie, Running government like a business has been a dismal failure, *The Globe and Mail*, 7 January 2013. The *Yes Prime Minister* series provides some examples too, albeit from a different take, my favorite being Leading Questions - Yes Prime Minister - YouTube.

In line with the more active policy role of the Conservative Party, this trend has resulted in a narrowing of public servant advice to issues of implementation, rather than broader ones of policy direction.[19] Within this context, perhaps the better question for practitioners is the degree to which the advice can be independent and "fearless." Public servants need to strike a balance in framing and timing their advice so that it will be considered, rather than dismissed. Herein lies the dilemma for public servants when a government has a radically different world view and evidence-base of issues and approaches. After all, it is not realistic to keep on giving advice contrary to the government's stated direction, even if that is what public service "expertise" suggests. "Fearless" is not the same as foolish, and therein lies the art and subtlety of the "considerations" section of most advice, whether oral or written, in signaling potential issues.[20]

As time goes on, this dilemma becomes less acute, as the policy parameters become clear when decisions are taken and the "loyal implementation" aspect comes into play. Part of this reflects a natural and healthy focus on implementation. Public servants cannot and should not continue to challenge ("re-litigate") once decisions are made, irrespective of the merits or weaknesses of those decisions. However, the political level with its understandable focus on implementation also needs to take care to preserve the space for "fearless advice" to ensure that decisions are as well informed as possible, including being aware of uncomfortable views and risks. In the end, of course, ministers and the government are responsible for their decisions.

But herein arises another dilemma: public servants risk internalizing the new orientation ("Stockholm syndrome"), and the quality of advice weakens as public servants, consciously or not, increasingly shape policy advice to be in line with what the political level wants to hear. Efforts to keep independent policy capacity and thinking are invariably diverted towards meeting deliverables, space for contrary views shrinks, and structural and personnel changes reinforce this internalization. After all, part of the challenge facing the Harper government was the resistance of public servants to its challenging of the previous bipartisan consensus on citizenship and multiculturalism, dating from the Trudeau years. As a result, public servants risked being perceived as neither professional nor impartial; opposition critics may view public servants as sycophants, and the handling of some files, such as the F-35 procurement, suggest the critics may be right.[21]

---

[19] See Lawrence Martin, The descent of democracy: A country under one man's thumb, iPolitics, 27 April 2011, and Donald Savoie (ibid), among others.

[20] One deputy minister characterized his approach to advice as follows: "while we have views, as long as it's legal, we will do it." In providing advice, there is a degree of truth to the Yes Minister dynamic. Bureaucratic writing tends to break most, if not all, of George Orwell's six rules on clear writing in his Politics and the English Language essay.

[21] See former Department of National Defence Assistant Deputy Minister (ADM) Allan Williams' comments in F-35 procurement process 'manipulated', CBC, 5 May 2012. The contrary example is the resignation of Munir Sheikh, former Deputy Minister of Statistics Canada, who resigned when the government misrepresented Statistics Canada's advice on replacing the mandatory long-form census with a voluntary survey. Statistics Canada chief falls on sword over census, The Globe and Mail, 21 July 2010.

Policy Arrogance or Innocent Bias

Of course, as Preston Manning has noted, a similar risk exists for political parties relying too much on the public service for policy ideas and initiatives, making it important that parties ensure they have independent intellectual capital and capacity:

> Build and maintain your "democratic political infrastructure" — the intellectual capital generators for politicians, the training programs for political activists, and the political communications vehicles — when in opposition but continue to build and maintain it, outside of the civil service and through private donations, even after becoming the governing party.
>
> To fail to do so is to court eventual political collapse and impotence from which it may take years, even decades, to recover ...[22]

However, the Conservative Party may have a higher degree of "inoculation" against this risk, given its general suspicion of the public service and the Reform Party's roots as a protest against previous policy continuity. The July 2013 post-Cabinet shuffle controversy about a "friends and enemies" list, and the guide titled "Who to avoid: bureaucrats that can't take no (or yes) for an answer", suggests ongoing suspicion regarding the loyalty of public servants, after some seven years of being in power.[23]

In many of the citizenship and multiculturalism issues, the evidence-based recommendations of public servants were discounted in relation to what the Minister and his staff were hearing from extensive outreach with a wide range of communities, in addition to their political priorities and principles. At times, public service expertise was challenged (sometimes correctly) as not addressing some issues; at other times, public service advice may have been perceived as arrogant ("truth to power") or even disloyal.

While differences of opinion between the bureaucratic and political levels are normal, reflecting different perspectives, evidence sets, time frames, and networks, the gap in some of the citizenship and multiculturalism files was particularly large given the government's overall distrust of formal research-based approaches in favor of a "principled approach" to policy priorities.[24]

As both the political and bureaucratic levels worked through policy and program options in citizenship and multiculturalism, they learnt about each other's policy perspectives, evidence-bases, and sensitivities. A number of aspects presented themselves:

- Contrasting ideologies and perspectives: The Minister and his staff had very different approaches from the public servants on issues as diverse as racism, equality and

---

[22] Because one day, Tories, you'll be out of office too, *The Globe and Mail*, 11 January 2012.

[23] Cabinet shuffle 2013: new ministers given "enemy" lists, *The Toronto Star*, 15 July 2013, 'Enemies' list memo tells us fervour often trumps pragmatism in Harper's government, *The Globe and Mail*, 18 July 2013.

[24] For one of the better overviews and critiques, see Allan Gregg's 1984 in 2012 – The Assault on Reason, 5 September 2012.

16

accommodation. This reflected different evidence sets, personal experience and preferences, in addition to the normal bureaucratic inertia of sticking to previous approaches;

- Evidence versus anecdote: Officials relied excessively on large-scale surveys and other evidence that did not take into account, and effectively ignored, any input from the Minister's extensive outreach to the various ethnic communities. The bureaucracy's existing stakeholders were favoured, rather than including new ones identified at the political level;

- Different perceptions of risk: Practical assessments of the risks, or perceived risks, involved in different options. In general, officials were, appropriately, more cautious about potential risks, flagging possible unintended consequences; the political level questioned what they viewed as an overly risk-averse approach that in many cases left out political risks; and,

- Particularly in multiculturalism, a number of areas were viewed as either too sensitive or too complex for the government to address.

None of these were exclusive. Ideology influences which evidence is chosen, which evidence is considered valid, and different perceptions of risk. However, looking at a number of case studies under each aspect provides a useful framework to assess how the dynamic between the political and bureaucratic levels played out.

In addition, the transfer of the multiculturalism program from Canadian Heritage to Citizenship and Immigration further changed the dynamics and focus. Having one minister responsible for citizenship, immigration and multiculturalism, rather than separate ministers, has and will continue to reduce the attention paid to the long-term integration issues related to multiculturalism. Other factors included the dispersal of multiculturalism functions across the functional model of CIC, rather than the vertical, business line model of Canadian Heritage (PCH); and the reality of CIC's "centre of gravity" of immigration selection and visitor admissibility.

This book tracks this dynamic between the political and bureaucratic levels, and within the bureaucracy itself, through a number of key citizenship and multiculturalism files, as well as some files where political-level interest was limited or cautious. Officials in many cases were overly confident in their expertise, unaware of the extent of their biases, and were consequently not prepared for this challenge. By working through each file, officials had to learn how to strike the appropriate balance between "fearless" advice on what research, evidence, and analysis suggested, and "loyal implementation" of the government's priorities. In some cases, officials needed to be reminded of the requirement to be professional and implement government policy direction, whether or not they agreed with it; the alternative, if they could not live with their advice and expertise being ignored, was resignation. In the early days, when multiculturalism was part of Canadian Heritage, signals from the "centre" (particularly, the Privy Council Office) overly reinforced this tendency to question government policy direction, further complicating relations between the political and official levels.[25]

These dynamics are explored in the following chapters:

Chapter 2: Which Ideology Will That Be? looks at how the Conservative government applied its worldview to creating the new national narrative in its citizenship guide, *Discover Canada*, and related changes to citizenship ceremonies. The multiculturalism program was reshaped towards greater emphasis on integration among and between all communities, not just mainstream/ visible minority relations, and finding ways to deliver grants and contributions (G&C) funding that met Ministerial requirements.

Chapter 3: Would that be Evidence or Anecdote? captures the different perspectives on evidence between officials, who tend to rely more on social science and broad surveys, and the political level, where anecdotes, through a wide range of encounters with Canadians, have more of an influence. At the macro level, citizenship behaviours between Canadians and the foreign-born show no significant differences, yet anecdotes highlighted a number of issues. Racism and discrimination, while at one level overshadowed by the government focus on antisemitism, remained an issue, and drawing on extensive ministerial anecdotes and finding more persuasive practical evidence was a challenge.

Chapter 4: What is at Risk? And for whom? examines the different perspectives on risk between officials and the political level. For citizenship, the development of the new test to accompany *Discover Canada*, the lack of sound data, and tight timelines meant a considerable degree of risk in implementation. In the case of multiculturalism, the historical recognition program's differential treatment of various affected communities posed a number of potential legal and political risks.

Chapter 5: Some Gaps and Omissions focuses on two multiculturalism issues that were pursued more at the bureaucratic than at the political level: the Quebec model of multiculturalism, *interculturalisme*, and radicalization/extremism. Both issues involve a number of sensitivities at the official and the political levels.

Chapter 6: Machinery Change outlines the process and impact of the transfer of the multiculturalism program from Canadian Heritage to CIC in October 2008 from both political and bureaucratic perspectives.

Lastly, Chapter 7: So What Kind of "Yes Minister" Shall That Be?, summarizes managing, and learning from, the interface between the political and bureaucratic levels, with emphasis on the need for policy modesty.

Ironically, one aspect shared by both the political and bureaucratic levels is over-confidence and a lack of policy modesty. Just as the political level is certain about its policies and priorities,

---

[25] After a while, departmental officials learned to discount some PCO advice, as both the general advice ("watch the Secretary of State") and views on particular issues tended not to reflect where the political centre (i.e., Prime Minister's Office) was.

the bureaucracy is equally certain about its evidence and expertise. Such mutual certainty is an inherent part of the relationship, where the right of a democratically elected government to implement its policies clashes with the belief (some would say arrogance) of public service experts that they know best. In the end, of course, the public service has to respond to the policy certainty of the political level as part of loyal implementation. This lack of policy modesty happens on a number of levels:

- Inherent complexity: Neither level fully appreciated the degree of complexity of society, social issues, and social policy. In social policy — in particular the complexity of society, communities and individuals — the large number of factors at play and the wide variety of institutions where many of the issues play out make it hard to identify issues precisely and understand fully what the most effective policy and program levers may be.

- Incomplete evidence bases: At the political level, no matter how extensive the outreach, the range of anecdotes will invariably reflect the fact that some communities, and some individuals, are listened to or engaged more than others. For officials, social sciences and related research are inherently imprecise, and reliance on large scale surveys misses some of the more granular detail that emerges in political encounters with Canadians. Just as the political level's insights were incomplete, so too was the expertise of the public service experts.

- Over-confidence in forecasting: Despite unavoidable complexity and uncertainty, both levels tend to be over-confident in their ability to forecast the medium- and long-term impact of policy and program changes, as well as to be able to anticipate all the potential side effects of such changes. People may respond to policy changes in ways that surprise, given their assessment of incentives for following or breaking the rules.

This policy arrogance is particularly problematic in citizenship and multiculturalism, where the federal government is but a minor player in relation to other levels of government, and a wide range of public and private institutions influence how different groups interact in society. The federal government has a limited number of touch points with Canadians, given the role of provincial governments. These touch points are largely limited to the following:

- Citizenship and naturalization (namely the study guide, test and citizenship ceremony), after which the department had little to no interaction with Canadians, compounded by the absence of a federal role in education and thus civics and history education; and,

- Multiculturalism, the limited reach of public education programming, modest funding for grants and contributions projects, limited impact on other government departments, and in general the minuscule size in relation to other federal and provincial programming meant that results would always be modest.

In other words, many of the changes made, while significant in the context of the particular policy, were also subject to many other forces and influences that would limit their impact.

Chapter 2

Which Ideology Will That Be?

While we typically think of political parties as having particular ideologies, no one is immune to ideological biases and perspectives. How we respond to different perspectives, how we assess evidence, and how we react to particular language is rarely completely neutral. Public servants, despite their efforts to provide evidence-based, impartial advice, are not immune. Officials who work on economic files tend to be more conservative (in a small "c" sense) than officials who work on social policy. Similarly, within departments officials may be more attracted to certain files as being more compatible with their own perspectives and beliefs.

The sharper ideological edge and different orientation of the Conservative government compared to previous governments challenged many public servants to recognize some biases of their own.

In many ways, all players involved — ministers, staffers, officials, academics, media, pundits, pollsters, etc. — share a certainty that their views are correct. This circle of arrogance makes the resolution of policy deliberations more difficult, as each player finds it difficult to acknowledge the limitations of his or her understanding and the influence of ideological and other biases. Such difficulties emerged when the department rewrote the citizenship guide, *Discover Canada*.

CITIZENSHIP: THE NEW NATIONAL NARRATIVE — *DISCOVER CANADA*

The Problem

In previous governments, citizenship had largely been a secondary interest for ministers. Early on in his tenure, Minister Kenney indicated his interest in revamping the citizenship guide for new Canadians (then *A Look at Canada*) and citizenship ceremonies:

> Legally speaking [citizenship] gives people status in Canada and certain rights like voting, but I think we need to reclaim a deeper sense of citizenship, a sense of shared obligations to one another, to our past, as well as to the future. In that I mean a kind of civic nationalism where people understand the institutions, values and symbols that are rooted in our history.[26]

---

[26] Interview in *Macleans*, 29 April 2009.

POLICY ARROGANCE OR INNOCENT BIAS

Much of this reflected conservative criticisms of both the substance and integrity of the citizenship acquisition process. _A Look at Canada_, the previous guide first issued in 1996, focused on the present, was light on history and democratic institutions, skirted controversial issues, focused more on rights than responsibilities, emphasized Canada's peacekeeping role, and, in the words of the Minister, had the wrong emphasis:

> Now, I'm all for recycling, don't get me wrong, but I'm even more for basic knowledge of the valued symbols and institutions of our country that are grounded in its history...[27]

The response was _Discover Canada_, a new guide that was detailed and thorough in depicting Canadian history, the role of our military in major world conflicts, the functioning of our democratic institutions, and the role of the Crown. In addition, it featured a more open characterization of Quebec,[28] acknowledgement of historical wrongs (ranging from residential schools to various immigration restrictions and wartime internment), and more muscular language to communicate Canadian values.[29]

If _A Look at Canada_ was overly grounded in the present, _Discover Canada_ was relatively light on contemporary Canadian history, whether regarding expansion of the social safety net (including medicare in the 1960s), peacekeeping, increased gender equality and human rights, the equality rights provision in the Charter, and gay rights.[30]

In parallel, citizenship ceremonies were adjusted to reinforce the new messages. The Charter was no longer distributed to new citizens, the ceremony guide folder _Our Citizenship_ highlighted a picture of the Queen, and 50 percent of the content of the insert _Becoming a Canadian Citizen_ pertained to the Crown and allegiance to the Queen. Serving the country through the military was highlighted, and it was silent on the equality provisions of the Charter (but mentioned core political freedoms of religion, thought, peaceful assembly, and association).[31] Military officers were now eligible to preside over citizenship ceremonies, and an effort was made to increase generally the visibility of the military and the RCMP during ceremonies.

---

[27] Speech by Minister, Canadian Chamber of Commerce Hong Kong, 13 September 2010.

[28] _A Look at Canada_ was issued shortly after the 1995 Referendum which may partly explain the avoidance of Quebec.

[29] E.g., "Canada's openness and generosity do not extend to barbaric cultural practices that tolerate spousal abuse, 'honour killings,' female genital mutilation, forced marriage or other gender-based violence." _Discover Canada_, Equality of Men and Women section.

[30] While the Minister had removed any reference to gay rights in the revision process of the 2010 edition (Immigration Minister pulled gay rights from citizenship guide, documents show, _The Globe and Mail_, 2 March 2010), pressure from Egale and others led gay rights to be incorporated in the 2011 edition (Gay rights referenced in new citizenship guide, _CBC_, 14 March 2011).

[31] See OB 182 – January 20, 2010, Use of new citizenship promotional products and directive for destruction of all old promotional material.

While Canada had traditionally prided itself on the fact that 96% of applicants became citizens, reflecting the emphasis on facilitation by previous governments, this statistic was viewed by the Conservative government as a sign that the test and process were too easy. With *Discover Canada* and its more comprehensive and complex content, any test would automatically be harder. Increasing the pass rate requirement from 60 to 75 percent was a further tightening. To improve the integrity of the test, a number of versions were randomly used because of accounts from some communities of answer sheets circulating among applicants.[32] While failure rates initially ballooned to 30%, further adjustments to question wording and the removal of mandatory questions allowed the target pass rate of 80-85% to be achieved.[33]

These changes were also accompanied by a series of measures to reduce fraudulent residency claims and further improve the integrity of citizenship.[34]

The Approach

Officials had grown up with the facilitative narrative, or making citizenship more accessible, a narrative that focused on modern Canada, with less interest in extensive historical accounts. While it was relatively easy to understand the Minister's criticism of the lightness of *A Look at Canada*, the challenge for officials was to understand and appreciate what was to them a different and largely unfamiliar perspective on Canada and Canadian history. But time to develop this understanding was compressed, given the need to deliver, in a relatively short period of 6 months, both a new guide and new test aligned to the government narrative.

To achieve the "deliverable" while ensuring adequate to-ing and fro-ing over content, three process mechanisms were implemented to ensure that the bureaucracy delivered on ministerial direction:

1. A Citizenship Action Plan (CAP) integrated the various elements of review and reform (*Discover Canada*, test, citizenship ceremonies) and provided a framework for weekly review of

---

[32] See *Agence France Presse* interview with the Minister, redistributed in 'Widespread cheating' in Canada citizenship tests, *Global Nation Inquirer*, 30 November 2010. The Minister is quoted as saying:

> The problem was the (old) citizenship test was passed by 97 percent of people, and there was widespread access to five standard sets of answers that people could buy on the market and cheating was widespread.

[33] Ibid. However, for some groups such as Afghanis and Vietnamese, failure rates remain high. See How applicants are stumbling on the final step to becoming Canadians, *The Globe and Mail*, 29 June 2012.

[34] See Speaking notes for the Honourable Jason Kenney, P.C., M.P. Minister of Citizenship, Immigration and Multiculturalism at a News Conference Regarding Citizenship and Immigration Fraud Investigations, CIC website, 10 September 2012. One unintended consequence of the increased integrity and other measures was that the backlog of citizenship applications increased 86 percent from 2007 to 2012, while citizenship applications only increased 30 percent from 2006 to 2012, meaning an increase in wait times from some 12-15 months to 23 months (Citizenship application process blamed for growing wait list, *CBC*, 23 April 2013).

issues and tracking of progress with the Minister's Office (MO). This was invaluable as, in contrast with the normal hierarchical and lengthy bringing of issues to the MO, it provided regular and immediate feedback, with issues being flagged to senior management (and presumably the Minister) as required. A further benefit is that this strengthened the relationship and understanding between officials and political staffers, while maintaining the distinction between the department and official levels.

2. While a formal bureaucracy/political interface issue, the *faux pas* of transferring the pen from officials to the Minister's Office to get an early draft aligned to the Minister's wishes actually helped officials understand what was wanted, which areas needed to be addressed, and the tone that was desired.[35] Initial review of the MO draft led to some tense discussions at first, as the focus and tone was so different from conventional official-level drafting. However, the frankness and openness of discussion allowed official-level concerns to be raised ("fearless advice") and, equally importantly, helped educate officials on the background and intent behind the new historical narrative. Following the MO draft and discussion, the drafting process reverted discretely to officials.

3. At the suggestion of the Deputy at the time, the Minister agreed to the creation of an informal advisory board, comprising a range of prominent citizens and academics, with the most active contributors sharing an interest in a stronger historical narrative.[36] While the members, taken as a whole, could be described as conservative leaning, they were not partisan and provided useful feedback, suggestions, criticisms and validation of the overall approach. [37] Unfortunately, given time constraints and the preferences of the Minister's Office, the "board" never met and discussed the draft as a whole. Officials, along with a ministerial staffer, conducted individual interviews with most members, and some exchanges by email with others. The Minister's Office may have also had some separate discussions with key members. A richer contribution would likely have resulted from more interplay and discussion among board members, rather than the individual interviews. Interestingly, while some of official-level concerns were picked up, many were not — another teaching moment for us as officials.

These process innovations were effective in facilitating the debates between CIC policy officials and their counterparts in the Minister's office. Three examples stand-out:

---

[35] Having an historian in the Minister's Office made this easier. Some might argue this point, but the staffer was clearly operating with the strong support of the Minister.

[36] Dr. Janet Ajzenstat, Curtis Barlow, Dr. Randy Boyagoda, Marc Chalifoux, General John de Chastelain, The Rt. Hon. Adrienne Clarkson, Andrew Cohen, Alex Colville, Ann Dadson, Dr. Xavier Gélinas, Dr. Jack Granatstein, Rudyard Griffiths, Dr. Lynda Haversack, Dr. Peter Henshaw, Dr. D. Michael Jackson, Senator Serge Joyal, Dr. Margaret MacMillan, Dr. Christopher McCreery, James Marsh, Fr. Jacques Monet, Dr. Jim Miller, Deborah Morrison, Dr. Desmond Morton, Bernard Pothier, Colin Robertson and Dr. John Ralston Saul.

[37] Citizenship guide edits reveal politics provides a summary of the comments of Board Members, *The Globe and Mail*, 17 January 2010.

1. Language and tone were discussed. While officials wanted simpler language, consistent with the basic language proficiency required by *The Citizenship Act* (Art. 5 (1) (d), defined in regulation as Canadian Language Benchmark Level 4, or basic fluency), the nature of the material, the depth of the history, and the preference not "to dumb it down" made the level of the guide in the CLB Level 7-8 range — fine for civics classes in Canadian high schools, more of a challenge for some applicants with relatively basic language knowledge. This was flagged, along with the likely groups that would be affected, including the impact on women. In the end, *Discover Canada* called for a significantly higher language comprehension level than the requirements of the *Act*.

2. Another debate was in the choice of the word "barbaric" to describe cultural practices that harmed women. Officials noted that while this term would resonate with many Canadians, it would be preferable to provide some broader context to the development of women's rights in Canada to help those communities understand better the Canadian context, rather than simply labeling other cultural practices as barbaric. In the end, the Minister preferred this more muscular language and considered this a useful media hook to highlight interest in the guide.[38] In subsequent interviews, the Minister further clarified his thinking:

   > "I'm not saying that wearing a niqab is barbaric. I am saying that the
   > whole citizenship process is an opportunity for us to instill in people a sense
   > of Canadian – read broadly, western liberal democratic – values, including
   > the equality of men and women," he said. "And I think most of us would
   > regard a … tribal practice forcing women to cover their faces illiberal."[39]

3. As the text of *Discover Canada* was finalized, one last flagging of major remaining issues of concern was the subject of a Deputy memo to the Minister. A number of issues were highlighted, with the major ones being the absence of the equality clause of the Charter and gay rights.[40] While the Minister, as is his right, did not accept this advice (save an explicit reference to gay rights and same-sex marriage in the subsequent edition), the issues were appropriately brought to his attention for consideration.

Interestingly, one of the unintended consequences of CIC's organizational structure (a functional model separating policy development from program delivery) was that the directions laid down in the new citizenship guide were more closely followed than changes to citizenship ceremonies. While there was integration at the general level (the Citizenship Action Plan process)

---

[38] As Justin Trudeau found out the hard way following the release of the second edition. See Justin Trudeau's honour-killing unease fans cultural-relativist flames in *The Globe and Mail*, 15 March 2011. Lysiane Gagnon made a stronger argument against such language in government publications (repeating her earlier critique) in 'Barbaric' is the wrong tone for an immigrant guide, *The Globe and Mail*, 10 April 2013.

[39] Jason Kenney wants to 'stop the madness' in immigration system, *The Globe and Mail*, 4 April 2012.

[40] See Immigration Minister pulled gay rights from citizenship guide, documents show in *The Globe and Mail*, 2 March 2010.

and the policy and operational teams worked well together, the above changes to the citizenship ceremony documents and procedures were not as high profile as changes to the guide and test. These were routed through a different ADM (Operations) and thus less subject to senior-level monitoring than some of the language in *Discover Canada* routed through the Policy Assistant Deputy Minister (ADM).

Once these remaining issues were addressed, the focus shifted to pre-production, the announcement of the new guide, and related supporting materials, including the official comparison between *A Look at Canada* and *Discover Canada*.

Overall, *Discover Canada* received high praise from a number of media and other commentators,[41] although it provoked some public debate regarding the overall messaging and tone, some of which had been anticipated in official advice, some not.

MULTICULTURALISM: FROM ACCOMMODATION TO INTEGRATION

The Problem
The Government's resetting of Canadian multiculturalism ethos began with Jason Kenney's arrival at Canadian Heritage as then Secretary of State of Multiculturalism in January 2007 and it continued following its shift to CIC and his becoming Minister of Citizenship, Immigration and Multiculturalism in October 2008.

The Minister had a dual mandate: a largely political one of engaging ethnocultural communities through extensive outreach, and secondly, one of reviewing the Multiculturalism program, in particular whether it was overtly political in its administration of grants and contributions.[42]

While the actions were meant more to reshape and redefine multiculturalism towards greater explicit reference to integration, the machinery change in 2008 marked the end of the standalone multiculturalism program and its incorporation into the broader citizenship, immigration, and integration agenda of CIC.

An illustration of the shift over time, comparing the 2004-5 priorities (under a Liberal government) to the 2010-11 objectives, following the full renewal of the multiculturalism program by the current government, is revealing:

---

[41]<u>Backgrounder — Comments about Discover Canada</u>, CIC, 14 March 2011.

[42] In fact, political "responsiveness" was built into the multiculturalism, as public education provides communications platforms for Ministers and the Grants And Contributions (G&Cs) program required Ministerial approval without delegation to officials, unlike, for example, settlement (language training) G&Cs which were delegated to officials.

Table 3: Contrasting Multiculturalism Priorities — 2004-5 to 2011-11

2004-05 Priorities	2010-11 Objectives
Fostering cross-cultural understanding	Building an integrated, socially cohesive society
Combating racism and discrimination Civic participation	Engaging in international discussions on multiculturalism and diversity
Making Canadian institutions more reflective of Canadian diversity	Making institutions more responsive to the needs of Canada's diverse population

The shift from understanding and accommodation to integration and social cohesion, the abandonment of racism and discrimination, greater consideration of faith-based communities, and the abandonment of civic participation, de-emphasized the "full and equitable participation" provisions of *The Multiculturalism Act* (Art 3.1.c). A further nuance was the highlighting of one form of racism and discrimination, antisemitism (now covered under "international discussions").[43] This reflected the concerns of the Canadian Jewish community, the attentiveness of the government to those concerns, and a number of related high-profile international activities and processes.

Much of the change started through the Minister's review of grants and contributions proposals.[44] Staff would work with non-governmental organizations to develop project proposals based upon existing — i.e., previous — government priorities. Not surprisingly — even if officials at the time were surprised — the Minister refused to sign most projects submitted.[45] While from a program management perspective, applicants had followed the rules and posted guidelines, officials did not fully appreciate the change in direction and orientation[46] and were not agile

---

[43] In 2009, Canada become a member of the International Holocaust Remembrance Alliance - IHRA (formerly called the International Task Force on Holocaust Education, Remembrance and Research). The Minister played a strong role in a number of international meetings on antisemitism, including the Ottawa 2010 Inter-parliamentary Coalition on Antisemitism. Domestically, hearings of the Canadian Parliamentary Coalition to Combat Antisemitism took place in 2010.

[44] As noted earlier, the multicultural program G&Cs have always been subject to Ministerial approval, not delegated, to provide the Minister with a more politically sensitive tool, even if the projects were developed and presented by officials.

[45] A large portion of projects were refused by the Minister. The end result can be seen in Appendix D - Lapses in Multiculturalism Program G&Cs, where over 50 percent of program funding lapsed in fiscal years 2009-10 and 2010-11, before the introduction of the new Inter-Action multiculturalism G&C program implementation late in 2010. This eventually became public in 2013 (see Millions in federal multiculturalism funding goes unspent each year, *The Ottawa Citizen*, 30 June 2013).

[46] The kind interpretation. Some wishful *Yes, Minister* thinking was another element.

enough shifting gears. Amusingly, in retrospect, the Minister's Office would double-check the applicant's background by Googling them; the use of language such as "white power" and the like by an organization was a warning flag that it was unlikely to be "directionally aligned."

While the Minister's extensive outreach activities were seen to be driven largely by political objectives, they also meant that he could challenge any analysis or recommendation by officials, by noting that a particular issue or concern was not on the agenda or among the priorities of those with whom he had been meeting.

The Approach

Once again, for officials who had grown up under *The Multiculturalism Act* and the previous bipartisan consensus, this change in orientation came as a shock. The concrete manifestation was the challenge by the Minister and his staff to G&C project proposals which were submitted by departmental officials for sign-off.

This took place at a number of levels:

- Staff, who worked with non-governmental organizations (often the same ones for many years), demonstrated the initial stages of the Kübler-Ross grief model, particularly denial, anger and depression. How could the Minister not approve a project proposal that had been signed off by all levels? How could the Minister possibly know better than we experts what the concerns of the communities were? How could the Minister challenge providing another grant to the same organization for a comparable project? What should we do now if our expertise and counsel are simply dismissed?

- Management, also in the same initial Kübler-Ross stages, recognized the prerogative of the Minister to approve or reject projects (after all, no Minister had ever delegated multiculturalism G&Cs approval to officials). However, they were concerned about the process. The program guidelines and priorities were published, applicants and staff had submitted project proposals in good faith, and it was unfair to have them rejected as the new program objectives and priorities had not been published and promoted. Rejecting fully compliant and meritorious funding submissions ran counter to everything officials had been taught about good program management. Senior management flagged to the Minister possible negative public attention to the high refusal rate, a theoretical concern as it turned out given that no groups raised this publicly and it passed completely under the radar.

Officials tried to find different ways to respond to the new directions. In retrospect, while these reflected progress to the "bargaining" stage, there were still elements of denial and depression. From the political perspective, this was likely viewed as more akin to disloyalty and a biased public service, rather than psychological trauma. But the end result was an adjustment process by both the political and bureaucratic levels that took time and a number of efforts:

- **Policy framework — Phase 1:** To provide clarity to applicants and to staff, new priorities and objectives needed to be developed. While this would not help existing projects in the pipeline, it should, at least going forward, ensure new projects were aligned with the Minister's policy direction. Rather than proceeding by drafting a Memorandum to Cabinet (the formal process for policy change), senior bureaucrats and MO staff held regular meetings and discussions. The debates around the priorities were started in 2007 and completed the following year, delaying a formal policy decision on taking multiculturalism in new directions. Nonetheless, the discipline of putting something down on paper forced rigour on both sides, and helped each have a better sense of what was wanted as well as how to capture this in a readable and understandable manner.

The priorities, intended to apply to G&Cs primarily, announced in February 2008, were:

> Supporting economic, social, and cultural integration of new Canadians and cultural communities;

> Facilitating programs such as mentorship, volunteerism, leadership, and civic education among at-risk cultural youth;

> Promoting intercultural understanding and Canadian values (democracy, freedom, human rights and rule of law) through community initiatives, with the objective of addressing issues of cultural social exclusion (parallel communities) and radicalization.[47]

- **Policy Framework — Phase 2:** While initially the department had a narrow focus of coming up with priorities that would help the management of the G&C program, there was a need to formally codify the Government's change in direction through a Memorandum to Cabinet. Following the program's transfer to CIC, officials undertook a broader review, encompassing all aspects of multiculturalism. The earlier process by which officials and political staff had developed the priorities, a more comprehensive sense from the Minister in a variety of fora, and associated files like citizenship gave officials strong direction to develop and argue for the objectives outlined above. While some of the initial discussions between officials and political staff were intense, these helped clarify the issues and directions.[48] The final objectives that emerged, to be applied across all multiculturalism activities, were as follows:

> Building an integrated, socially cohesive society, by promoting intercultural understanding, fostering citizenship, civic memory and pride, and respect for core democratic values, and promoting equal opportunity for individuals of all origins;

---

[47] "The way forward," <u>Annual Report on the Operation of the Canadian Multiculturalism Act 2007-2008</u>.

[48] The most amusing example, in the discussion of the "international discussions" objective, was a remark by one political staffer (not without merit) that the purpose of this objective and related activities were to provide officials with excuses to travel. Officials pointed out that international discussions included their priority on holocaust awareness and antisemitism (e.g., the International Holocaust Remembrance Alliance, the various international antisemitism initiatives), at which pointed it was accepted.

> Improving the responsiveness of institutions to the needs of a diverse population, by assisting federal and public institutions to integrate multiculturalism into their policy and program development and service delivery; and,

> Actively engaging in discussions on multiculturalism and diversity at the international level, by sharing Canadian approaches to diversity while contributing to an international policy dialogue on issues related to multiculturalism.[49]

The net change was a greater emphasis on integration, more explicit links to citizenship, and relative silence on racism and discrimination.

- **Operational:** In parallel with the policy framework renewal above, a number of steps were taken both within Canadian Heritage and subsequently at CIC to manage the program better and to ensure alignment to the emerging priorities. Within the Canadian Heritage context these included:

  - More in-depth examination of regional project proposals by national staff against the emerging priorities and advice on how to recast and redraft these. In many cases, this became a bit of a *Yes, Minister* exercise, as different words were used to describe projects that, at heart, reflected the old priorities and orientation, sometimes embarrassingly so. Officials were often caught out by political staffers who noted the language in the submission describing the organization, and contrasting that on the organization's own website.[50]

  - Regular sessions between officials and political staffers involved reviewing each project individually, and having informal discussions of the intent and background to the proposals. This also provided an opportunity to get feedback as to the reasons why any particular project had been refused by the Minister.

  - Efforts, ultimately unsuccessful, to develop a Ministerial sign-off mechanism that provided the option to refuse a project and space to list the reasons.[51] While the Minister may have understandably balked at providing written justification, his staff was generally forthcoming

---

[49] CIC Overview of the Multiculturalism Program deck, 2011.

[50] Language that the MO found particularly unacceptable included: white power, oppression, and racialized communities.

[51] One of the paradoxes of G&C etiquette is that the approval process only had space to sign "approved" and no space to indicate "refused." The rationale being that, at the bureaucratic level, the Minister should only see projects that have been approved by officials; at the political level, the rationale was less apparent. The weakness of the bureaucratic logic was revealed when officials were asked how many projects were refused by senior officials: no answer could be provided because none had been rejected, the file just moved on and upwards. Eventually, at both Canadian Heritage and CIC, senior officials did exercise more due diligence and refuse a number of projects, flagging these refusals to the Minister's Office, none of which were overturned.

in highlighting some of their concerns. In the early days, this was more like staff knowing what they didn't like and being less able to articulate what they did like.

- Following the transfer to CIC, a whole new layer of project review was put into place, ranging from the substantive to the silly. From a substantive perspective, CIC had little to no experience with this model of G&Cs, as virtually all settlement programming (language training and the like) had been delivered through what were effectively service contracts, rather than community development-type projects. Senior management had to understand the program and become comfortable with this different approach to G&Cs, and this took time. On the redundant side, more time seemed to be spent in placing each project submission in a new style of docket, adding nothing of substance, and causing significant delays in processing as the relevant briefing unit had to perform this essentially useless task.[52]

- In the end, none of these efforts made any difference in increasing the proportion of approved projects. At one ministerial meeting at CIC in 2010, the Minister walked through the list of projects submitted, making pointed remarks about why particular projects were not aligned to his priorities, after which senior management at CIC also started to refuse more projects in order to demonstrate greater due diligence and compliance.[53]

- **Change Management**: One of the major challenges was to bring staff around to these changes. Many multiculturalism staff had an activist orientation, one that had fit the program well during previous governments, but was no longer appropriate (if ever) for officials delivering government programs. Whether in the Canadian Heritage context, where such activism was more in keeping with the departmental culture, or at CIC, where a more conventional bureaucratic program delivery mindset prevailed, getting staff to change their attitude around the new priorities and then objectives was an ongoing struggle. The following change-management strategies were implemented:

  - Ongoing, weekly review of projects in relation to the new priorities and update on Ministerial feedback and direction;

  - Help in drafting (and redrafting) project submissions;

---

[52] A less fond memory is an angry phone call from the then Deputy accusing me of holding up the project files. He somewhat calmed down when I told him my service standard was two days turnaround, and the delay was within his own office and procedures.

[53] While this caution was warranted, in many cases these decisions reflected a need, on the part of officials, to demonstrate greater due diligence (and avoid the unpleasantness of another similar session with the Minister!) rather than the merits or lack thereof the project in question. In dealing with projects in Quebec, some officials felt that projects in Quebec were less deserving, given that immigration and integration funding and responsibility had been transferred to that province. Most Quebec-based multiculturalism projects were not supported at the senior official level and did not advance to review by the Minister. Unfortunately, from the perspective of broader federal presence, this was an example of typical individual departmental myopia in that it ignored one of the two levers available to CIC in Quebec (the other being citizenship).

- Management-level discussions between National Headquarters (NHQ) and the geographic regions to sensitize regional management and engage them in providing similar direction to staff;

- Regular visits to each region to provide regional staff with more direct opportunity to learn about the nature of the changes;

- A session with a number of multicultural staff (both regions and headquarters) to outline the changes and allow for more fulsome discussion of staff concerns and questions; and,

- Participation of the Minister in each of these sessions. To his credit, the Minister was generous with his time and engaged fully in the questions.

So large was the gap between the policy changes and the inertia of program staff that, in the end, none of the above strategies were helpful. Whether consciously or not, this reflected a failure of the bureaucracy, and appeared as disloyalty to the government. Ultimately, given that all else had failed, a machinery solution was applied: take the program staff completely out of the project development loop and shift to a more conventional Call for Proposals (CFP) approach in 2010. Suddenly, the problem of not having enough new projects developed in cooperation with staff morphed into the first CFP having over 700 submissions.[54]

Ministerial messaging in the Annual Report on the Operation of the Canadian Multiculturalism Act evolved in parallel with the Ministerial priorities and direction. The contrast between the previous government's messaging and the 2010-11 Report captures the change (Appendix E provides a fuller account):[55]

---

[54] This was also combined with a new "Events" stream to respond to smaller, community initiatives. It was a rare reversal of his previous criticism of "food and festivals" funding but responded to what he was hearing in his outreach, the need for a "retail" element to the program, to use the Minister's term. Notwithstanding this shift and alignment to the Minister's priorities, the program continued to have ongoing underspending; only 25 percent of recommended projects were approved by the Minister, with program spending of 63 percent of available funds. Millions in federal multiculturalism funding goes unspent each year, The Ottawa Citizen, 30 June 2013.

[55] Minister Chan's message largely follows the terms of the Multiculturalism Act, likely reflecting more bureaucratic input than in the more focused message on Ministerial priorities of Minister Kenney.

Table 4: Contrasting Ministerial Messaging 2003-04 and 2011-12

2003-04 Liberal: Minister Chan	2011-12 Conservative: Minister Kenney
Embracing and managing diversity is a distinguishing characteristic	Participation of all Canadians, not just newcomers
Combat discrimination, promote cross-cultural understanding, and make Canadian institutions more representative	Deepen understanding of the values, history, institutions, rights, and responsibilities that unite us as Canadians
Contribute to the continuing evolution of our country	Intercultural and interfaith understanding, shared values, civic pride, and our commitment to a peacefully pluralistic society
Data collection and research programs	Inter-Action and Community Historical Recognition
More inclusive society	Black History Month and role in War of 1812
Charter of Rights and Freedoms	Upcoming International Holocaust Remembrance Alliance Canadian Chairmanship
Equality of opportunity	Engage governmental and community partners.
Diversity as a source of strength and innovation	
Economy, culture, and society benefit when Canadians of diverse backgrounds share talents, perspectives, and experience	
Way of life … value at the heart of our collective identity	
Belief that diversity is synonymous with success, prosperity and the future.	

In many ways, the new direction of the multiculturalism program reflected a more up-to-date interpretation of multiculturalism, one adapted to the increased diversity within our major urban centers, where relations between communities are as important as the old "mainstream"/visible minority distinction. While the focus on removing barriers, racism and discrimination was largely overshadowed by the focus on antisemitism, the broadening to inter- and intra-community relations was clearly a needed and overdue change.

Chapter 3

Would that be Evidence or Anecdote?

Reading Daniel Kahneman's *Thinking, Fast and Slow*,[56] his book summarizing his years of research on automatic versus more deliberate thinking, and some of the traps of the former, provoked me to reflect on the contrast between political and bureaucratic decision-making. In general, ministers and their staff draw heavily on anecdotes, stories and what "people on the ground" are saying, with the impressions largely formed under what Kahneman calls System 1 (automatic thinking). A professional bureaucracy draws on more impersonal, large-scale studies and research, or evidence-based policy, to have a wider base of information (Kahneman's System 2, or deliberative thinking).

Of course, many politicians, including Minister Kenney, in developing their political approach, have taken a reflective intellectual journey to arrive at their ideological worldview.[57] Many officials, despite selecting and citing large-scale studies as objective, have their own embedded System 1 influencing the procedural and methodological choices (see this clip from *Yes, Prime Minister* at about the one minute mark for an extreme version of this)[58]. Evidence can be consciously or unconsciously subverted by the confirmation biases that lead us to favour evidence that fits our belief system. The dynamic between Kahneman's two systems is common to all of us; our System 1 automatic thinking is influenced by our deeper reflections, and our System 2 deliberative thinking is influenced by our experience and bias. Most of us are not conscious of how and why we make choices and decisions, from either perspective. From our own perspectives, we are all objective!

The legacy of Trudeau's brand of citizenship and multiculturalism, implicitly accepted under Mulroney, and reiterated under Chrétien/Martin, was to some extent internalized as the *de facto* paradigm.

In both citizenship and multiculturalism files, officials referred to their evidence base which, while solid, was overly comfortable and reflected the priorities of earlier governments as well as the internalized beliefs and biases of officials. Faced by ministers and political aides insisting that

---

[56] Daniel Kahneman, *Thinking, Fast and Slow* (New York : Farrar, Straus and Giroux, 2011).

[57] His first foray into politics was working for the Saskatchewan Liberal Party, including a stint as Executive Assistant to then-provincial-leader Ralph Goodale in 1988.

[58] "The Prime Ministerial Broadcast", *Yes Minister*, http://www.youtube.com/watch?v=oLhFXkvugLM

none of this resonated with what they were hearing in their interaction with a wide range of Canadians, officials had to rethink and develop a refreshed evidence base.

Just as policy making by anecdote and personal experience can lead to bad policy (readers from any country can likely find a few examples), policy that ignores anecdote and apparent popular opinion for the more formal broader evidence base risks missing its target objectives as well.

Officials had to accept anecdotes as part of the evidence, and learn how to integrate these into their research and analysis.

CITIZENSHIP: LIMITS TO EVIDENCE

The Problem

As will be discussed later in Chapter 4, CIC had not invested in generating any serious data and analysis of Canadian citizenship beyond operational and administrative statistics, unlike the comprehensive data sets and analysis related to immigrant selection.[59] In Chapter 4, I will outline how this played out in terms of changes in the citizenship knowledge and language tests, and how officials had to accept the anecdotal evidence and integrate it into changes to the citizenship test and language requirements. In many cases, these anecdotes helped address long-term weaknesses in the integrity of the citizenship program.

At the macro level, most polling and other research showed little difference between attitudes of Canadian-born and foreign-born citizens.[60] For example:

---

[59] Out of the 31 data sets in the Government-wide Open Data website, 29 pertain to immigration-related data (e.g., permanent and temporary residents, humanitarian efforts) and only 2 pertain to citizenship (Appendix H). More comprehensive data sets and analysis for long-term integration issues, including citizenship and multiculturalism, are under development.

[60] From the 2012 CIC Departmental Performance Report:

Data comparable to that collected in 2010 is not available. Therefore, direct comparisons are not possible. However, a similar survey found that:

- 62% of Canadians felt that multiculturalism is good for Canada;
- 88% of the foreign-born and 81% of the Canadian-born reported feeling "very proud" to be Canadian;
- 41% of the foreign-born and 33% of the Canadian-born reported that good citizens "obey laws"; and
- 12% of the foreign-born and 8% of the Canadian-born reported that good citizens vote.

The foreign-born continue to demonstrate that their level of attachment to Canada exceeds that of the Canadian-born and that their understanding of what is required of citizens is superior to that of the Canadian-born.

- Similar views on what makes a good citizen (obeying laws, actively participating in the community, helping other people, being tolerant of others and sharing or adopting Canadian values);[61]

- Similar voting participation rates;[62]

- Comparable sense of belonging to Canada;[63]

- Minor differences on immigration levels and Canadian values;[64] and,

- Comparable volunteering and charitable donation rates.[65]

In other words, despite the weaknesses in citizenship testing, language proficiency and other integrity issues, at a macro level Canadian immigration, citizenship and multiculturalism policies showed comparable civic behaviours between Canadian and foreign-born, and could be considered largely successful. However, anecdotal evidence from a number of communities, and the inherent limitation on the ability of macro-level studies to shine light on possible differences between communities, suggested that these studies did not tell a complete picture. Officials were not aware of any studies that separated out citizenship behaviours by community (in contrast to other socioeconomic data such as income, employment and incarceration levels by community, which was more available). To a certain extent, officials had to accept ministerial anecdotes as part of the evidence-base, given Minister Kenney's more extensive outreach, and the lack of studies at the needed level of granularity.

Another example where the anecdotes "trumped" the evidence was in the case of "birth tourism," in which visitors to Canada would plan their arrival in order for their child to benefit from current Canadian regulations that granted citizenship to any child born on Canadian soil (*jus soli* or citizenship determined by place of birth). Limited hard data existed on the extent of the problem; the Minister admitted that he did not know the extent of the problem even as he made the case to crack down on birth tourism:

---

[61] Immigrants the proudest Canadians, poll suggests, *CBC*, 15 February 2012.

[62] *Canadian Election Studies* (1988, 1993, 1997, 2000 and 2004) and data from the *Ethnic Diversity Survey*.

[63] Second-generation Canadians had a higher sense of belonging to Canada (88 percent) compared to first generation immigrants (81 percent) and the general population (79 percent). Ipsos-Reid survey for the Historica-Dominion Institute, Becoming Canadian Study Results, 2 March 2007.

[64] *The National Post/Forum* survey, using either/or questions, showed 70% supported limits to immigration, 58% of Canadians born in another country, and 66% of second-generation Canadians. A more nuanced survey by the Association of Canadian Studies showed the majority of Canadians (59%) were not worried about the number of immigrants in Canada. Of those born in Canada, 55% were not worried, compared to 71% of those not born in Canada. Most Canadians in favour of limits on immigration: poll, *The National Post*, 10 March 2013.

[65] *2007 Survey of Giving, Volunteering and Participating - Imagine Canada*, 2009.

> We don't want to encourage birth tourism or passport babies … This is, in many cases, being used to exploit Canada's generosity. The vast majority of legal immigrants are going to say this is taking Canada for granted.
>
> We need to send the message that Canadian citizenship isn't just some kind of an access key to the Canadian welfare state by cynically misrepresenting yourself. … It's about having an ongoing commitment and obligation to the country.[66]

Officials struggled with this lack of hard numbers as stories emerged in the Quebec and BC media, the former about the Maghreb and the Middle East, the latter regarding Chinese "birth tourism."[67] Surprisingly, reliable statistics were not easily available publicly, notwithstanding that hospitals likely had this information given the administrative systems in place to capture medicare-compensated medical services versus privately-paid services. Some media coverage showed that the scope of the issue was minimal — about 0.1 percent of total live births in 2005.[68]

Subsequently, CIC engaged in consultations with a range of medical associations and hospitals to ascertain the extent of the issue. Not surprisingly, these consultations revealed more evidence of birth tourism than previously known, as well as identifying some additional groups where birth tourism appeared to be practiced.[69]

Unfortunately, this evidence, while stronger than before, remains at the level of informed anecdote. It is surprising that CIC did not, or was not able to, consult with the provincial medicare systems. After all, the larger ones have sophisticated billing and payment systems that should allow extraction of relevant data regarding paid births (through medicare) and unpaid births (e.g., permanent residents of Canada within the three-month waiting period for medicare coverage, visitors to Canada including birth tourism). Such analysis would help quantify the extent of the issue, and help inform cost-benefit analysis of any change to citizenship legislation

---

[66] Minister Kenney from Power and Politics interview, quoted in *CBC* article 5 March 2012 http://www.cbc.ca/news/canada/story/2012/03/02/birth-immigration-citizenship.html.

[67] Minister Kenney quoted in "Tory crackdown on 'birth tourists' will eliminate Canadian passport babies," *National Post*, 5 March 2012. http://news.nationalpost.com/2012/03/05/passport-babies-canada/.

[68] See *Immigration Watch Canada*, 8 March 2009, showing some 273 births to foreign mothers in Quebec and 169 in the rest of the country in 2005-06, out of a total of some 335,000 births - that's about 0.13 percent. See http://www.immigrationwatchcanada.org/2009/03/08/quebec-docs-report-rise-in-baby-tourism-but-furious-when-foreigners-skip-on-bill/, *The Canadian Press*, 8 March 2009.

[69] 'Birth tourists' believed to be using Canada's citizenship laws as back door into the West, *The National Post*, 10 August 2013.

to align Canadian policy with other jurisdictions that no longer allow automatic citizenship upon birth.[70]

While the increased two-way flow of immigrants, brought about by globalization, cheap travel and changing economic opportunities provides a policy case for reviewing *jus soli*, this needs to be balanced against the realistic extent of the problem and the costs involved in administering a more complex citizenship regime, likely at both the federal and provincial levels, given the links between citizenship and vital statistics.

MULTICULTURALISM: DISCRIMINATION OR RACISM?

The Problem

As a follow-up to the controversial Durban UN World Conference Against Racism of 2001, the Canadian government implemented Canada's Action Plan Against Racism (CAPAR) in 2005. CAPAR was a mix of packaging existing programming across 20 departments and the addition of incremental funding of $53.6 million for 9 new initiatives in Canadian Heritage (where the Multicultural Program was then housed), CIC, Human Resources and Skills Development, and Justice. There was weak horizontal coordination, and over time the initiatives evolved according to the priorities of the respective departments and successive waves of reallocating resources to new priorities.[71]

At the same time as CAPAR was coming up for evaluation and renewal, the Minister was sending a number of signals regarding his overall approach to racism and discrimination issues:

• Distrust over the various UN processes related to racism, discrimination and human rights, exemplified by the government pulling out of the follow-up conferences to the Durban UN conference;[72]

• Skepticism over large-scale surveys, such as the 2002 Ethnic Diversity Survey (EDS), which showed comparatively high levels of self-reported racism, prejudice, and discrimination;[73]

• Aversion to any terms like "white power," "racialized communities" or equivalent language, particularly among organizations applying for grants and contributions;

---

[70] Only Canada and the United States, among developed countries, grant automatic birthright citizenship.

[71] See the CAPAR evaluation by CIC in 2010. http://www.cic.gc.ca/english/resources/evaluation/CAPAR/summary.asp.

[72] See speech by Minister Kenney At the Perils of Global Intolerance Conference, New York, New York, 22 September 2011.

[73] See Ethnic Diversity Survey: portrait of a multicultural society, Statistics Canada, 2003.

Policy Arrogance or Innocent Bias

- Concern over racism, prejudice and discrimination among and within ethnic communities, not just between the "mainstream" and visible minorities;

- Greater acknowledgement and awareness of religion as a legitimate part of multiculturalism and diversity, and more extensive outreach to the various religious communities in Canada;

- Rejection of employment equity, expressed publicly in a case involving a CIC competition, leading to a government review of employment equity in federal government hiring;[74]

- Odd language in annual press releases on the International Day for the Elimination of Racial Discrimination (21 March, the anniversary of the Sharpeville massacre in South Africa), raising the question of what would be "just" racial discrimination:

  > That is why our Government has pledged its unwavering commitment to preventing unjust racial discrimination from becoming a deep and systemic problem in Canada.[75]

---

[74] Tories take aim at employment equity - The Globe and Mail, *The Globe and Mail*, 22 July 2010:

> "We can continue to achieve greater diversity in the public sector without prohibiting people from applying for jobs on the grounds of their race or ethnicity," Mr. Kenney said. "It's a very simple principle and I think it's something the vast majority of Canadians would appreciate."

[75] Minister Kenney issues statement recognizing the International Day for the Elimination of Racial Discrimination, 21 March 2012. No one questioned — or noticed — this language in political or media comment. By 2013, they had got rid of that odd language, and were largely silent on traditional racism and discrimination issues, replacing them with language focusing on religious or faith-based discrimination:

> The International Day for the Elimination of Racial Discrimination is an opportunity for Canadians to join with other freedom-loving people around the world in reaffirming our commitment to reject and eliminate all forms of racial discrimination.

> While we can be proud of our own country's successful pluralism, we need to ensure that all Canadian citizens reject extremism, do not import ancient enmities, and continue to embrace Canada's tradition of ordered liberty, which guarantees the equality of all citizens under the law.

> Through initiatives such as the Office of Religious Freedom, our Government will also continue to condemn acts of racial hatred around the world. These acts often accompany the targeting of religious communities.

> As Minister of Citizenship, Immigration and Multiculturalism, I encourage all Canadians to continue to uphold the fundamental values of our free, democratic and peacefully pluralist society and to reject all forms of unjust discrimination.

Minister Kenney issues statement on the International Day for the Elimination of Racial Discrimination, 21 March 2013

- Sensitivity to the concerns of individual communities, such as the Chinese Canadian community's concerns about assaults of Chinese Canadian anglers at Lake Simcoe in 2007, and yet being careful about how to comment, if at all;[76]

- A preference for activities and events which were easier to tailor to the government's messages, such as Black History Month[77] and Asian Heritage Month, rather than the general racism and discrimination messaging of the Mathieu Da Costa or National Video Competition student-oriented competitions;

- Creation of the Paul Yuzyk Award, tailored to the integration theme, recognizing a Conservative pioneer of multiculturalism, and appropriating multiculturalism as a Conservative, rather than Liberal, initiative;[78]

- Emphasis on Holocaust awareness and antisemitism rather than general racism and discrimination issues; and,

- More attuned to the practical concerns of the suburban ethnic communities, and less so of the downtown activists that traditionally had worked with the Multiculturalism Program.

As noted in Chapter 2, one practical result of these concerns was the high refusal rate of grants and contributions multiculturalism projects, as these reflected previous government priorities, and not the new emphasis. As a result, some $5 million in "enhancement funding" under CAPAR for the multiculturalism program was reallocated towards other departmental priorities and expenditure reductions.[79]

The Minister was also sending strong signals as to the relative importance or weight that the government attached to the various communities, including faith-based communities, through his governmental and political outreach. While there is no publicly available list of the innumerable

---

[76] Bizarre assaults hit quiet town, *The Toronto Star*, 26 September 2007. See Secretary of State Kenney Responds to Alleged Attacks on Asian Canadians, 5 October 2007:

> Canadians have built a diverse society based on mutual respect and peaceful co-existence. However, recent events remind us all that we can never take this achievement for granted, and that we must always be vigilant against hatred inspired by race, religion, and ethnicity.

[77] For example, the theme of the 2008 Black History Month was the 175th anniversary of the abolition of slavery throughout the British colonies, combining the themes of history, British heritage, and the Black experience in Canada. Canadian Heritage: Secretary of State Kenney Launches Photography Exhibit for Black History Month

[78] Paul Yuzyk was a Manitoba Senator, appointed by PM Diefenbaker in 1963, who served until 1986. In his maiden speech in the Senate, he made one of the early references to multiculturalism and has thus been dubbed the "father of multiculturalism." Speaking notes for the Honourable Jason Kenney, 12 June 2009. As noted earlier, the Ukrainian Canadian community was particularly influential in making the case for multiculturalism.

[79] Given that the program had not managed to spend any of the enhancement funding, this cut was more theoretical than practical.

community and other events the Minister attended, the public record of official speeches and statements from 2007-11 is revealing:[80]

Chart 3: Ministerial Outreach by Community

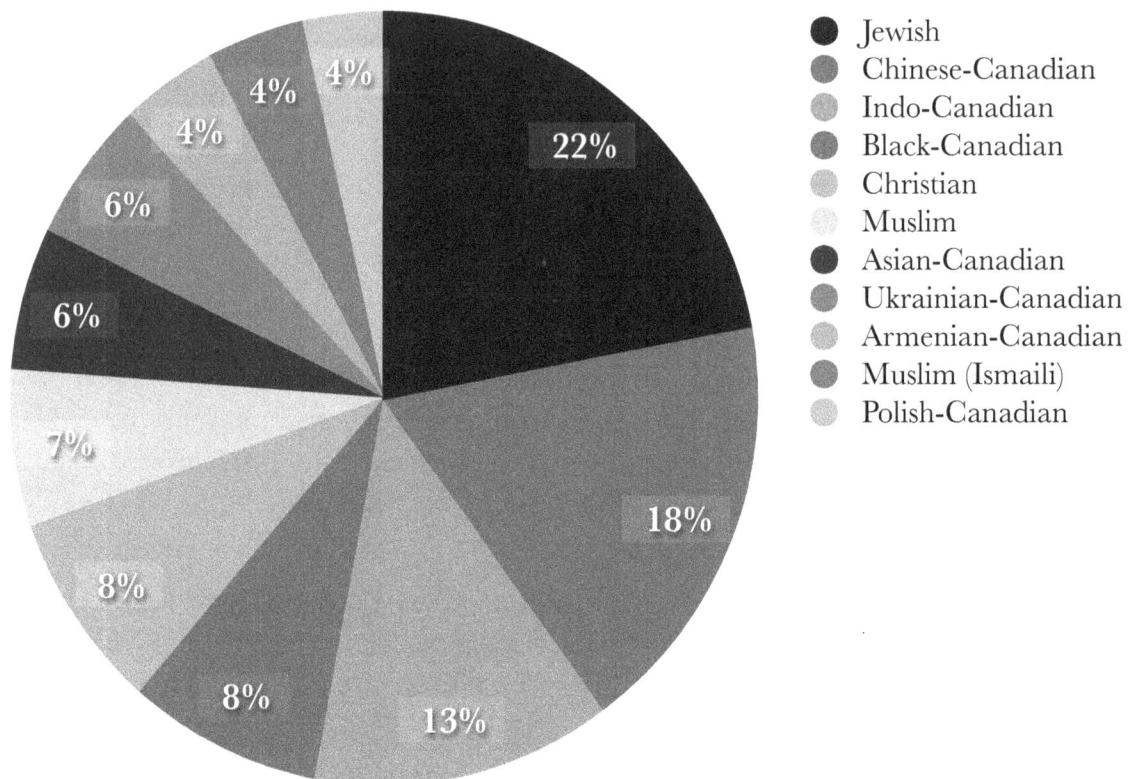

Legend:
- Jewish
- Chinese-Canadian
- Indo-Canadian
- Black-Canadian
- Christian
- Muslim
- Asian-Canadian
- Ukrainian-Canadian
- Armenian-Canadian
- Muslim (Ismaili)
- Polish-Canadian

Pie chart values: 22%, 18%, 13%, 8%, 8%, 7%, 6%, 6%, 4%, 4%, 4%

[80] This chart understates the degree of outreach and communities spoken to as it only includes those events or statements for which official speeches or statements were prepared by the government (some 270 from 2007-2011). Some speeches or statements may not have been included in the web archives. Methodological notes:
- Sources: CIC and Canadian Heritage (at Library and Archives) websites.
- This chart does not include speeches and statements with a general audience (49) or other communities (55), both of which account for 38 percent.
- When both speech text and statement issued, counted separately.
- "Others" include communities with less than 1 speech or statement per year (see Appendix C for details).
- 2008 statements from Canadian Heritage missing.

The political strategy has been summed up as the "fourth sister" of Canadian politics. See Tom Flanagan's Courting the Fourth Sister, *The Globe and Mail*, 13 November 2008.

The Approach

Officials remained in the initial Kübler-Ross stages of denial and, to some degree, anger that the traditional approach to racism and discrimination issues was not accepted and no longer adequate to capture the concerns and interests of the Minister and his staff. While much of this contrast of views between officials and political staff manifested itself in the process of drafting speeches and statements, and in the discussions over multiculturalism grants and contributions projects discussed in Chapter 2, the question of what to do with Canada's Action Plan Against Racism (CAPAR) remained, particularly as the time approached for the standard five-year evaluation requirement. It became evident that the approach of CAPAR was not in sync with the government's priorities.

At one level, not much had to be done. The horizontal coordination process among lead (PCH, CIC, HRSD and Justice) and other departments was junior-level, one with no decision-making authority, as the design of the horizontal initiative had been largely to provide a CAPAR "umbrella" over a number of existing and incremental initiatives. No one would really notice the absence of interdepartmental coordination: there was little to begin with. As noted earlier, departments had already reallocated CAPAR-related program funding to other programs or to meeting expenditure reduction requirements. The Multiculturalism Program was no exception; along with cutting the "enhancement funding," the staff who were managing horizontal coordination were increasingly diverted to supporting Canada's membership bid for the International Holocaust Remembrance Alliance and related initiatives combatting antisemitism. CAPAR was not on the radar of the Minister, as long as current material reflected the government's priorities and approach.[81]

But letting CAPAR die a slow death without defining what could be an appropriate approach reflecting the government's orientation was not viable, given that CAPAR-type language remained across a number of government websites and how intrinsic racism and discrimination issues were to the Canadian Multiculturalism Act.[82]

Officials had to learn to listen to — and respect — the key messages and insights coming from the Minister, reflecting his anecdotes and conversations from his extensive community outreach. In other words, getting beyond the denial stage was the first step, and surprisingly difficult for many. Bargaining was tried without success, as noted earlier, in the case of grants and

---

[81] While in early years, the Minister would make reference to CAPAR, and it provided a useful "soundbite" in House Cards to respond to questions on what the government was doing, references to CAPAR became less useful and frequent as time went on. Canada's response to the Universal Periodic Review in 2009 was silent on CAPAR.

[82] Canadian Multiculturalism Act - Lois du Canada - Justice, particularly, 5 (1) (g): "assist ethnocultural minority communities to conduct activities with a view to overcoming any discriminatory barrier and, in particular, discrimination based on race or national or ethnic origin."

contributions projects. Nor were officials successful, in the early days, in their attempts to suggest more "moderate" language for speeches and statements.

Part of the problem was that the traditional evidence amassed by officials, drawing on large-scale surveys such as the 2003 Ethnic Diversity Survey, did not resonate with the Minister or his staff. Whether it was justified or not, officials had to find other kinds of evidence beyond general surveys, evidence that would resonate more with the messages that the Minister was hearing through his outreach. Given the Minister's (and the government's) general skepticism about social policy research, the need to find convincing, practical evidence demonstrating ongoing racism and discrimination in Canada challenged officials who came primarily from a social policy background, and who saw the existing methodologies and approaches as unimpeachably reliable.

Officials started with a number of national and regional roundtables to test out some themes that responded to the Minister's views. These results were surprising to the expert officials. In contrast to some of the reactions from longtime multiculturalism staff, the recurring recommendations from discussions were largely compatible with the proposed new direction, and included:

• Expand the racism and discrimination strategy to include interfaith initiatives;

• Make targeted interventions for specific groups when needed;

• Include focus on relationship between Aboriginal peoples and newcomers;

• Address tensions between and within ethnocultural communities; and,

• Use positive language (move away from "antiracism") — emphasize commonalities rather than focusing on differences.

At the early stages, an additional issue emerged within CIC. The long history of race-based immigration restrictions — the Chinese Head Tax, the "continuous journey" clause,[83] restrictions against Jewish immigration, and others — has been well documented, with these restrictions being lifted in the 1960s as Canada moved to a "colour-blind" immigration policy. However, some of the formative experience of CIC officials comes from their experience abroad, much of which takes place in countries where immigration fraud is widespread. This influences their perspectives, whether consciously or not. Within CIC, there was skepticism that racism and discrimination remained serious issues in contemporary Canada.[84] Given the need for any proposed approach on racism and discrimination to gain approval at various levels within CIC, getting past the bureaucratic obstacles was the first challenge.

The initial Citizenship and Multiculturalism Branch proposal, which focused on some of the broad surveys and related evidence, was shot down at CIC's Policy Committee in late 2010.

---

[83] The 100th Anniversary of the Continuous Passage Act, CIC, 29 October 2008

[84] One example being an early discussion at Policy Committee (the first level in the approval process), when one senior official essentially said: "I don't see racism and discrimination as being an issue."

Officials regrouped and proceeded on a number of levels to strengthen the analysis and substantiate the argument for action regarding:

- Hate Crimes: The hate crimes statistics compiled by Statistics Canada (the National Standardized Data Collection Strategy on Hate-Motivated Crime Initiative) were considered the most reliable statistics available, as these reflected hate crimes reported to police (i.e., not just self-reported in a survey).[85] The hate crimes statistics had the advantage of highlighting antisemitism, one of the government's priorities, while including other groups subject to hate crimes and discrimination. While the statistics likely reflected under-reporting from a number of groups, they were credible and had been compiled for a number of years.[86]

- Correlation: Drawing on work of Michael Orenstein,[87] officials compiled the cumulative evidence of different outcomes by religious and ethnic communities in the following tables. While these did not prove causality — were these difference in outcomes caused by racism and discrimination? — they did demonstrate a strong correlation between ethnic origin, economic disadvantage, discrimination, settlement challenges and diaspora politics. Taken together, the difference in outcomes across a range of income and social indicators helped to demonstrate some of the cumulative challenges experienced by a number of groups, and suggested a link to racism and discrimination.

---

[85] Police-reported hate crime in Canada, 2011, Statistics Canada, 17 July 2013

[86] For a detailed analysis of the statistics, see Police-reported hate crime in Canada, 2010 from Statistics Canada. As some groups are more comfortable reporting hate crimes (e.g., Jewish Canadians, given the work of organizations like B'nai Brith), newer communities such as Muslim-Canadians may under-report.

[87] See Ethno-Racial Groups in Toronto, 1971-2001 - A Demographic and Socio-Economic Profile, Institute for Social Research, 2006.

Table 5: Ethnic Community Specific Challenges[88]

Visible Minority Group (% Total Population)	Economic disadvantage		Discrimination (% hate crimes based on race/ ethnicity)	Settlement Challenges for Foreign-Born and Immigrants (2001-2006)		Diaspora Politics, Inter-Community / Imported Conflicts
	Unemploy. Rate	Low-Income Incidence*		Foreign-born	Immigrants	
Non-Visible Minority	6.2%	12%	N/A	12%	1.2%	European conflicts
Black 2.5 %	10.7%	29% (62% Somali)	40%	71%	15.6%	Somalia Gang violence
Aboriginal 3.8 %	13.9%	17%	3%**	N/A	N/A	Gang violence
Arab /West Asian (WA) 1.3 %	12.1%	39% (48% Afghani; 21% Egyptian)	9%	83% (Arab) 92% WA	31.2% (Arab) 40.5% WA	Middle East Afghanistan
Chinese 3.9 %	7.5%	28%	8%***	82%	17.2%	Human rights Tibet, Enclaves
South Asian 4.0 %	8.5%	21%	12%	84%	22.7%	Sri Lanka India/Pakistan
Latin American 1.0 %	9.0%	28%	N/A	80%	24.7%	N/A

---

[88] Drawn from background analysis, Programming to Address Discrimination, fall 2010. Notes as follows:
* Low income incidence is based on percentage below Low Income Cut-Off, population 15 and over, 2006 Census.
**Hate crimes against Aboriginals may be under-reported due to the unavailability of data.
***East and Southeast Asian.

46

Table 6: Religious Group Specific Challenges[89]

Visible Minority Group	% of population	Economic Disadvantage (% of families earning less then $30k/year)	Discrimination (% experienced hate crimes based on religion)	Accommodation Issues	Diaspora Politics, Inter-Community/ Imported Conflicts
Control Group: Christians	74.8%	16%	N/A	Hutterites photo ID issues	European conflicts
Muslims	2.7%	36%	16%	Niqab & burqa issues (voting, language classes)	Middle East, India/Pakistan, Somalia, 9/11 and related
Jews	1.1%	10%	65%	Hasidim issues ("YMCA")	Middle East
Sikhs	1.2%	26%	N/A*	Kirpan and turban issues	Punjab
Buddhists	1.1%	27%	N/A*	N/A	Tibet
Hindus	1.2%	25%	N/A*	N/A	India (internal)

- Blind CVs: Once this general correlation was established, it was harder for officials to dismiss racism and discrimination as possible causes for differing outcomes and greater integration challenges. Still, officials needed evidence of practical barriers to participation. The most convincing example found was the blind CV test, whereby researchers would submit identical CVs, controlling for education and experience, but with different names. The results were striking: Canadians with foreign-sounding names were 40% less likely to be called back for a job interview than those with identical resumes and non-foreign (English) sounding names. In the words of Professor Oreopoulis, who conducted the study:

> Unfortunately, the study shows an applicant's name matters considerably more than his or her additional education, multiple language skills and extracurricular activities.[90]

- The commulative effect of hate crimes statistics, correlation of outcomes with ethnic origin or religion, and the blind CV test helped at both the official and political levels to demonstrate that racism and discrimination were ongoing issues. The tables were particularly helpful at the next meeting of CIC's Policy Committee, allowing the deck to continue to subsequent approval levels.

---

[89] Drawn from background analysis, Programming to Address Discrimination, fall 2010. Note: *Statistics Canada does not include Sikhs, Buddhists or Hindus as categories for hate crimes motivated by religion. These would be captured in the category of other religion-motivated hate crimes, which rose from 5% in 2007 to 14% in 2008.

[90] From Right résumé, wrong name, *The Globe and Mail*, 20 May 2009.

POLICY ARROGANCE OR INNOCENT BIAS

- Although not formally part of a proposed new approach to racism and discrimination, the emphasis of the government on antisemitism and Holocaust awareness, or focus on the concerns of particular interest to Jewish Canadians, provided opportunities for officials to link this targeted approach to the possibility of other initiatives targeted to other communities.[91] In other words, rather than the general racism and discrimination messaging of the past, this area could be broadened to include specific community initiatives, linked under a wider theme.[92]

- To further address any remaining objections from senior officials, as well as to pave the way for ministerial approval, diligent drafters systematically combed through Ministerial speeches and statements for relevant quotes, largely anecdote-based, and scattered them liberally throughout the deck. A number of the most helpful:

> I do acknowledge the ongoing reality of racism in our society. I suspect that it is something that will never be eliminated. It is something that we can hopefully, as a society, diminish over time and we should make every reasonable effort to do so...[93]

> And my primary concern in this regard ... is that as Canada maintains the highest relative levels of immigration in the world, ... we find increasingly that the most virulent and sometimes violent forms of xenophobia raises intolerance and prejudice come and are experienced between new Canadians who come from the same country or region of origin.

> When I visit a Sufi mosque in Montreal that has been vandalized, they claim, by members of a Wahhabi mosque down the street, that concerns me. When I visit a Sinhalese Buddhist monastery that has been firebombed by local residents, probably new Canadians from the same

---

[91] Not all recognized the broader implications. One official referred to these initiatives from a narrow issue management perspective as "all things Jewish."

[92] There was an example at the Ottawa Conference of the Inter-Parliamentary Coalition to Combat Antisemitism (ICCA). The *Ottawa Protocol* made a broader reference to racism and discrimination, but unfortunately only in the section pertaining to universities:

> Working with universities to encourage them to combat antisemitism with the same seriousness with which they confront other forms of hate. Specifically, universities should be invited to define antisemitism clearly, provide specific examples, and enforce conduct codes firmly, while ensuring compliance with freedom of speech and the principle of academic freedom. Universities should use the EUMC Working Definition of Antisemitism as a basis for education, training and orientation. Indeed, there should be zero tolerance for discrimination of any kind against anyone in the university community on the basis of race, gender, religion, ethnic origin, sexual orientation or political position...

[93] Jason Kenney, Multiculturalism National Meeting, 2 June 2010.

country of origin, that concerns me. And when we see expressions of hatred directed at Jews in areas where that may be an ancient hatred coming forward newly in Canada, that concerns all of us. And so we must be very deliberate about ensuring that Canada's success in promoting diversity, pluralism and intercultural understanding continues in the future.[94]

We know that diversity is increasing in Canada and varies in its makeup from one region to another. This makes our jobs challenging and complex, so we must work hard to ensure continued social cohesion and focus on what unites us as a country.[95]

This strategy worked for getting beyond whether racism and discrimination continue to be issues in contemporary Canada, worthy of government attention. As to the question of what the government's role should be, the approach built on the themes of the Minister, while maintaining a strong racism and discrimination focus, but largely silent on any remaining "mainstream"/ visible minority discrimination. The themes included:

"Improving interfaith/intra-faith understanding;

Addressing tensions and pre-existing prejudices within minority communities; and,

Specific initiatives for targeted communities."[96]

To be provocative, officials also proposed an option that raised the question within CIC grants and contribution programs about the appropriate balance for short-term integration and settlement projects (i.e., language training) and the long-term integration issues addressed by multiculturalism projects. Officials proposed to shift a marginal amount of funds from short-term to long-term integration. At that point, multiculturalism project funding amounted to $10.9 million; settlement projects received close to $1 billion.

Much to everyone's surprise, this option survived as the preferred option at all internal review stages. This was surprising, as it argued for a small funding reallocation from settlement to multiculturalism. While even the Minister was comfortable with the idea of reallocation, this was

[94] Jason Kenney, Inter-parliamentary Coalition for Combating Antisemitism Conference, 9 November 2010.

[95] Jason Kenney, Multiculturalism National Meeting, 2 June 2010.

[96] Overview of the Multiculturalism Program deck, 2011.

not implemented given the need to review all demands on access to settlement funding,[97] which became subsumed into CIC's preparations for government-wide spending reviews.[98]

To demonstrate just how this approach would be different, officials used the standard before/after approach:

Table 7: Comparison Between Current and Proposed Programming[99]

What we are doing now	*What we want to do in the future*
Responding to first World Conference on Racism in Durban, South Africa (2001)	Align with evolution in government's approach to addressing discrimination
Broad horizontal approach but with a diffuse and weak impact	Critical mass of capacity within CIC to generate a more measurable impact
"One size fits all" programming	More targeted, evidence-based initiatives that address specific challenges facing communities at higher risk of discrimination
Limited interfaith programming	Address emerging issues in interfaith/intra-faith understanding
Limited programming aimed at imported conflicts and imported discrimination	Address tensions and pre-existing prejudices within minority communities
Heavy focus on short-term integration programming (99% versus 1% for long-term)	More balanced approach to building an integrated, socially cohesive society

The strengthened policy analysis of the proposed new approach, which had an easy time in the Policy Committee and Executive Committee, was the subject of an equally easy discussion with the Minister's Office (there is little that is more effective at trumping bureaucratic and Ministerial staffer reserve than using a Minister's quotes), and met with the Minister's approval. Although someone posed the question of whether it should go before Cabinet as an information item was contemplated to let Cabinet know that CAPAR was formally "dead," the Minister decided that this was not necessary. When officials later suggested a Deputy letter to communicate this to other departments, primarily HRSD and Justice, their recommendation was overtaken by the election call in spring 2011.

Ironically, while getting this through the system was a major achievement as there were no pull factors from the political level, some multiculturalism officials noted correctly that the new approach abandoned the traditional focus on mainstream/minority issues and neglected the

---

[97] Foreign credential recognition initiatives were also seeking access.

[98] Earlier reviews had reduced integration/settlement funding by 5% or $53 million for FY 2011-12, making reallocation more challenging.

[99] Working Draft, Programming to Address Discrimination, fall 2010.

provisions of the *Canadian Multiculturalism Act* on removing barriers.[100] However, the new themes kept analysis and language on racism and discrimination, expanded the issue beyond mainstream/minority relations, and further brought faith issues into discussion of these issues, while recognizing the need for differentiated approaches based on community needs.[101]

---

[100] *Canadian Multiculturalism Act*, sections 3.1.c and 5.1.g.

[101] When officials organized a quick celebration following the approval of the new strategy, a number of staff who had worked on the initiative did not attend, given their concerns over the new orientation.

Chapter 4

What is at Risk? And for Whom?

Political and official levels have different perceptions of what constitutes risk in policy development and implementation. Officials seek to ensure that advice reflects risk assessment from the legal, policy, program and service aspects. They tend toward caution, partly to counter-balance anticipated political perspectives, which from the standpoint of elected officials are the very thing that got them elected.

In addition, in their effort to exercise due diligence, officials may over-emphasize theoretical risks without fully taking into account the probability of any particular risk occurring. The political level may, in turn, tend to discount official level risk assessments as overly cautious. The difference in the short-term political risk of not meeting government commitments may differ significantly from the medium- and long-term risks identified by officials. The result is considerable differences in perceived and, in some cases, actual risk. [102]

CITIZENSHIP: IMPROVING PROGRAM INTEGRITY

The Problem

There were strong policy and program administration rationales for improved integrity of the citizenship program, along with the government's policy choice to make the knowledge requirements more demanding through *Discover Canada* and the associated knowledge test. Integrity refers to the department's confidence that its decisions are accurate, well-informed, and reality-based, with strong fraud prevention measures.

Integrity applies to three major levels: knowledge, language, and residency. The citizenship program had in the past boasted about the 96 percent success rate of applicants becoming new

---

[102] E.g., legal challenges to new policies take time to weave their way through the courts and formal program evaluations take place only every five years, meaning the full consequences of program changes in many areas will only be seen many years after changes were implemented.

citizens (the Minister signaled early on that he was more comfortable with an 80-85 percent success rate)[103]. The high success rate reflected a number of factors:

- As noted earlier, the simpler *A Look at Canada* and associated test that only required 60 percent to pass;

- No systematic rotation of test versions to reduce the potential for sharing of questions and for memorization of answers.[104] The actual test was paper-based, and no analysis beyond raw scores was available;

- Language skills were informally assessed in initial discussions with applicants when they came in to write their citizenship tests. If an applicant made it through that screening (essentially reviewing basic application information, testing basic oral language skills), and successfully passed the test (testing basic reading skills), they were deemed to have met the language requirement. Anecdotally, the Minister would recount too many cases of Canadian citizens without adequate basic knowledge of either English or French, which made him wonder how well language was being assessed.[105]

- Citizenship judges reviewed any applicants that either failed the initial screening or the knowledge test. Under previous governments, the instruction to the judges had been more to err on the facilitative side; the new emphasis on integrity required judges to apply greater stringency to their applicant interviews and gave them some standard tools to use.[106]

- The review of residency requirements was not thorough, and had been complicated by a range of judicial interpretations of what "residency" meant, ranging from the common sense "Tim Horton" test of being physically present to the consultant interpretation, to legal residency proven by a mailing address, and filing taxes.

The accumulated impact of these factors reflected inadequate attention to the integrity of the citizenship-granting process[107] and facilitated the high acceptance rate. The challenge was to have a better sense of what the impact on the acceptance rate would be as each of these control factors was tightened in turn. While much of the focus was on the bottom line acceptance rate,

---

[103] Later confirmed by Karen Shadd, then CIC media spokesperson, quoted in Citizenship-test failures skyrocket, *CBC*, 28 November 2010.

[104] One anecdote circulating in the Chinese Canadian community was that there existed a mnemonic song linking each question to its answer, e.g., 1a 2c 3a etc.

[105] The Minister, on his frequent international travels, would hear anecdotes from a number of Canadian ambassadors regarding the need to provide consular services to Canadian citizens through interpreters because many did not have an adequate knowledge of either English or French, meaning that the language requirements of citizenship clearly had not been met.

[106] Citizenship Language Screening Tool, Operational Bulletin 246, 30 November 2010.

[107] The 2011 Audit of the Citizenship Program section of risk management, among others, outlines — gently — some of the weaknesses in the integrity of the program.

having a better sense of which communities would be more affected, and whether women or men would be more affected, was helpful in reviewing the possible role of settlement programming in helping the more affected groups prepare for the test.

From a policy and program perspective, part of the challenge was the lack of detailed data and analysis of the application process, particularly the citizenship test. CIC had no integrated citizenship database, unlike the extensive immigrant database that allowed for detailed analysis across the various data sets.[108] Officials did not know which knowledge questions were problematic, there was no systematic information available on which groups (by country of birth) failed to meet the language requirements, and the tight timelines for the desired changes meant that a certain amount of flying blind was required.[109]

The Approach

In developing policy and program advice, the paucity of data and analysis made it hard to provide advice on the likely impact of any policy changes. Moreover, the Minister's wishes for early implementation meant there were limits to appropriate due diligence. While in changes to language requirements, this understandable rush was tempered by regulatory requirements, in other areas, like the knowledge test, operational considerations were more of a constraint. Starting with the knowledge test within these constraints, a number of steps were taken:

---

[108] See CIC 'Facts and figures' or the Open Data website data (CIC Datasets). The only citizenship statistics available are the operational "Administrative Data Release," essentially files processed or being processed, in addition to the Top 10 Source Countries (Appendix F and Appendix G respectively). Or, as noted earlier, only 2 of 31 datasets produced by CIC. Some of this data exists but is not made public (e.g., CIC Citizenship Management Quarterly Report), in contrast to immigration data (e.g., processing times, provincial and urban area breakdown, approval rates), other data was not collected at the time (e.g., pass rates by country of birth). See Appendix H for the complete list of CIC datasets, showing the under-investment in citizenship. Australia, in contrast, publishes a wide range of citizenship statistics, including approval rates by country of birth for the top 10 source countries.

[109] Citizenship tests are paper-based, and only the result (pass/fail) was recorded. Moreover, at the time, the results were not tracked in the CIC operational database, making analysis by country of birth or identification of problematic questions difficult.

POLICY ARROGANCE OR INNOCENT BIAS

1. To address the lack of data, officials, working with Statistics Canada, put into place a separate manual survey to collect and analyze results from the new tests. While not ideal — officials were live testing new and different material without focus testing — this analysis was invaluable on three levels: [110]

    a. Identification of vulnerable groups who encountered particular difficulties with the test. Not surprisingly, education level was the main predictor of pass rates, with some communities more affected than others, and in some cases, marked gender gaps; [111]

    b. Identification of particular questions where high numbers of applicants did not answer correctly. This allowed officials to suggest alternate wording to make the question more easily understandable, without changing the intent or purpose behind the question; [112] and,

    c. Removal of the mandatory questions, or those few questions that must be answered correctly, irrespective of the overall test score. It became clear from the analysis that the combined effect of more difficult content, a higher pass rate requirement, and mandatory questions resulted in a pass rate lower than the target of 80-85 percent.

2. During the implementation of the new test, interim results were shared with the Minister's Office every two weeks. This was at the aggregate overall pass rate level, broken down by Canadian region, rather than detailed demographic (age, gender, country of origin) and question-by-question analysis.

---

[110] Officials, at the policy, operational and communications levels, pressed for focus group testing to identify question wording issues. General and ideological resistance to focus group testing ("what will it tell us that we don't already know") meant a higher initial failure rate than desired, and provided a harder hurdle particularly for those groups with a weaker grasp of sophisticated English. (The French version of the test scored better initially; perhaps the translators had improved on the original language in some cases.)

Some informal focus group "testing" did take place, however. I tried out the new test versus the old test with my then teenage children, who both aced the old test, whereas only one (barely) managed to pass the new one. More significantly, we ran a mock test at a policy sector retreat with several hundred policy analysts, providing a reasonable proxy for most Canadians' level of citizenship knowledge — most failed.

[111] Applicants from countries with less than 60 percent succeeding in 2011 included: Afghanistan, Burma, Cambodia, Dominican Republic, Equatorial Guinea, Guinea-Bissau, Laos, Somalia and Vietnam. Most of the countries with 60-80 percent success rates were in Africa. Map: How immigrants scored on Canada's citizenship test, *The Globe and Mail*, 29 June 2012.

There were also significant gender differences in a number of countries, largely attributable to differences in education levels, although not noted in media coverage. Section 5: Gender-based Analysis of the Impact of the Immigration and Refugee Protection Act, 2011.

[112] Given an ongoing Ministerial Office sensitivity to "dumbing down" language in the guide and test, hard data on questions where high numbers of applicants were not answering the question correctly focused attention on those questions where the wording or formulation was not clear.

3. During the implementation phase, and to compensate for being part of a live focus test group, any applicant who failed was given a second chance to write the test.[113]

Unfortunately, it appears that history has repeated itself. The new 2012 versions of the test, likely without focus group testing or detailed information on a question-by-question basis (i.e. how applicants fared with each question), had the predictable result of causing an increase in test failure. From 2011 to 2012, the failure rate rose from 17% to 27%.[114]

Changing language requirements was more complex. The language requirement ("adequate knowledge") and the role of citizenship judges in making the final determination were referenced in legislation. Any changes needed to follow the normal regulatory processes (*Canada Gazette* pre-publication requirements, and associated timelines).[115] This was in contrast to *Discover Canada* and the revised knowledge test, where CIC had broad regulatory authority along with existing policy authority, and had no need for public consultation and pre-publication.[116]

From an operational perspective, CIC had long wished to make language assessment more efficient. The preferred approach of having language assessed along with the initial application, upfront as it was, should, it was thought, help reduce processing time and backlogs. In contrast to the largely policy-driven changes in knowledge requirements, changes in language requirements were also motivated by operational needs, as part of an overall effort to modernize the citizenship business processes and operations.

As always, implementing the changes involved a number of steps:

1. Settling on an operational definition of what "adequate language" meant in practical terms. In contrast to the question of knowledge, the issue was not to change the requirement but

---

[113] Subsequently, in June 2013, the government announced the possibility for applicants to have a retest within a number of weeks to reduce the general citizenship backlog and the requirement for hearings with a judge. CIC News Release — Improving the Citizenship Application Process, 3 June 2013. See Appendix F for citizenship processing statistics, showing the dramatic increase in the processing backlog in 2012.

[114] More people failing revamped citizenship tests, *CBC*, 14 June 2013. It is likely that this reflected Ministerial Office direction, although this time without the justification of the time pressures of a minority government. An example of how a political decision, stemming from an aversion to focus group testing and standard processes, can impact implementation, undermining the sound policy intent of improving citizenship test integrity.

At one point in time, officials had suggested the development of a tablet-based electronic test and analysis system to improve program integrity through greater randomization of test questions and provide more detailed test data and analysis at the individual question and country of birth level. However, given more fundamental citizenship processing issues and resource constraints, this was understandably dropped. Other countries such as Australia have put in place comparable systems to address data and analysis needs.

[115] Language assessment included the right to see a citizenship judge, and this role was enshrined in legislation. Citizenship Act - Part V - Procedure.

[116] See TBS Guide to the Federal Regulatory Development Process.

simply to define it more rigorously. Officials settled on <u>Canadian Language Benchmark 4</u> (CLB 4), essentially the advanced beginner stage (or "fluent basic proficiency"), meaning language ability adequate to function in basic life and work situations.[117]

2. Addressing the legislative requirement that allowed applicants to have their file reviewed by a judge, whether or not they had submitted proof of language capability. Initial legal and policy advice could not find a way to do this given the strong authority of the judges designated by the *Act*.[118]

3. However, in a second iteration (motivated by a difficult ministerial meeting in fall 2010 ("What do you mean you can't do this?")), officials become more creative, and interpreted the requirement to have the file reviewed by a judge as not precluding administrative measures that could separate applicants into two streams. Applications with language assessment would proceed; applications without would be returned. Any returned application could be resubmitted for review by a judge, but it would be at the back of the queue. The speed of processing was used as an incentive to encourage up front language assessment. A clever work-around, but not without legal risk.

4. While work was taking place to define an adequate measure of language capability, a number of sessions were held with citizenship judges to improve the level of consistency in their assessment of language to the level of CLB 4, along with related standard procedures and tools for both citizenship officials and judges.[119]

5. Finding the right balance between practical measures of language assessment and rigorous assessment took some time, but it was not difficult. Common sense prevailed: if the department already had proof, or the applicant had previously undergone standard testing, Canadian educational experience, or had participated in Canadian language training, that would be sufficient. The result, now in effect, was remarkably unchanged from some of the initial thinking:

---

[117] See <u>Centre for Canadian Language Benchmarks</u> for the individual benchmarks.

In contrast to the study guide, where everyone could (and did) have opinions as to what elements should be included in the "national narrative," the more specialized nature of language competencies left less room for debate and more reliance upon outside expertise. The Minister's office had historical expertise, not language expertise, another contributing factor to the relative lack of debate and discussion over the appropriate language level. *Discover Canada*, ironically, was written at a level more like CLB 7-8.

[118] *Citizenship Act* Article 14 (1).

[119] <u>Operational Bulletin 246 – November 30, 2010</u>, Implementation of the New Language Screening Tool in the Citizenship Process.

Table 8: Language Assessment and Equivalencies

Measures of Language Assessment and Equivalencies
Third-party test results already provided to CIC or Ministère de l'Immigration et Communautés Culturelles Québec (MICC)
New third-party test results, including any one of the following: • CELPIP General (Canadian English Language Proficiency Index Program General test) • CELPIP General-LS – a two-skills (listening and speaking) version of the CELPIP General test • IELTS – General training (International English Language Testing System) • Test d'Évaluation de Français (TEF) (in French only) • Test d'Évaluation de Français adapté au Québec (TEFAQ) (in French only) or TEF épreuves orales – a two-skills (listening and speaking) version of the TEF.
Proof of completion of a secondary or post-secondary education program in French or English, in Canada or abroad
Proof of achieving CLB 4 in speaking and listening through a Language Instruction for Newcomers (LINC) course or proof of achieving CLB/NCLC 4 in speaking and listening issued by a provincially funded language training course in Manitoba, British Columbia or Quebec.

- The normal regulatory process required pre-publication, comment, and adjustment as appropriate. In other words, the standard checks and balances in the regulatory process, in contrast to the development of *Discover Canada*, helped ensure greater due diligence in the development of the new approach and a more measured approach to implementation, including more advance notice to applicants. The Regulatory Impact Analysis Statement noted a net monetized cost of $1.7 million, primarily for additional language training and time for applicants to meet the language requirements, balanced against increased employability of permanent residents who "enhance their language skills at an earlier stage."[120]

- Some other checks-and-balances, such as the User Fee Act, which requires any changes to user fees, or to the specific scope of services provided, to be subject to a number of process and publication procedures.[121]

---

[120] "Regulations Amending the Citizenship Regulations," *Canada Gazette*, Volume 146 no. 16, 21 April 2012.

[121] See TBS website, User Fees.

MULTICULTURALISM: THE CASE OF HISTORICAL RECOGNITION

The Problem

Successive governments have grappled with the issue of historical recognition, or how to recognize events in Canadian history that, while legal at the time, are no longer in keeping with contemporary values and laws. From a legal perspective, recognizing past wrongs, whether wartime internment or immigration restrictions, is distinct from admitting guilt or liability and thus being open to legal claims.

By default, officials tend to be uncomfortable with such files. Calls for historical recognition, while reflecting historical injustices, also represent the respective strength and influence of the particular communities as much as the historical events themselves. Moreover, officials may have tended not to distinguish sufficiently between all potential risks (small and great) and the probability of the risk being realized. But potential risk can be mitigated with a better understanding of some of the political dynamics. Just as the political level has to acknowledge risk assessment by officials, officials have to acknowledge some of the political risk management insights of the elected representatives.

Additionally, while officials have to look at the risks particular to historical recognition, the political level has to take into account the broader perspective of government-wide strategy. This is not only in relation to narrow electoral considerations with respect to attracting support from a number of ethnic communities, but equally to pave the way for more ambitious and controversial immigration and related reforms. It was easier for the government to tighten immigration and refugee policy when they acknowledged the excessive restrictions of the past. "Playing ethnic politics," in other words, was likely a means to the broader policy renewal.

The main claims presented to governments over time included Japanese Canadian World War II internment, the Chinese Head Tax of 1885-1923, Ukrainian Canadian World War I internment, Italian Canadian World War II internment, the "continuous journey" restrictions 1908-1947 against Indian immigration, and restrictions against Jewish immigration in the lead-up to and during World War II.

Traditionally, Liberal governments resisted such claims. Prime Minister Trudeau's line, "I do not see how I can apologize for some historic event to which we... were not a party,"[122] was maintained by the Chrétien government. In 1994, Sheila Finestone, Secretary of State (Multiculturalism) and Secretary of State (Status of Women), stated:

> Seeking to heal the wounds caused by the actions of previous
> governments, six ethnocultural communities have requested redress and
> compensation totaling hundreds of millions of dollars. The government

---

[122] http://asia-canada.ca/new-attitudes/fairness-and-tolerance/apology.

understands the strong feelings underlying these requests. We share the desire to heal those wounds.

The issue is whether the best way to do this is to attempt to address the past or to invest in the future. We believe our only choice lies in using limited government resources to create a more equitable society now and a better future for generations to come.

Therefore the government will not grant financial compensation for the requests made. We believe our obligation lies in acting to prevent these wrongs from recurring. The government will continue to take concrete measures to strengthen the fabric of Canadian life by combating racism, prejudice and discrimination through education, information and the promotion of the values of fairness.[123]

Conservative governments were more flexible. The Mulroney government successfully negotiated the Canadian Japanese Redress Agreement in 1988, including *ex gratia* payments of $21,000 to some 18,000 survivors, a public apology by then Prime Minister Mulroney in the House of Commons, and the creation of the Canadian Race Relations Foundation, with an initial endowment of $24 million, as a means to reduce future racism-based measures.[124]

However, these positions became less firm over time. Just before it fell, Paul Martin's Liberal government developed the Acknowledgement, Commemoration and Education (ACE) program in 2005. The ACE provided "initial funding" of $2.5 million to the Chinese Canadian, Italian Canadian and Ukrainian Canadian communities for projects to mark their historical experience, all large, well-established, and politically active communities.[125]

While the Reform Party had largely been silent or opposed to historical recognition,[126] the newly formed Conservative Party targeted ridings with large minorities for whom redress

---

[123] *Hansard*, 35th Parliament, First Session, 9066.

[124] See Canadian Race Relations Foundation Act, 1991.

[125] Who will pay for Canada's victim industry?, Jeffrey Simpson, *The Globe and Mail*, 17 December 2005.

[126] See Tom Flanagan's op-ed, *The Globe and Mail*, 21 March 2012, essentially reiterating the position of former Prime Minister Trudeau:

> …recognition of what we now see as past wrongs can be in order, but apologies ring false unless they are made by those who actually committed the injustice. You apologize to people when you've been mean or thoughtless, but what good does it do for those who run contemporary governments to apologize for the actions of people in past centuries who acted in good faith under the law as it then was?

was important. As a result, the Conservatives supported the intent of the ACE program and, once in power, expanded its scope and funding.[127]

Development and implementation of the Conservative government approach started with the Chinese Head Tax program in 2006, providing, as in the Japanese Canadian model, symbolic *ex gratia* payments of $20,000 to those who paid the head tax or their spouses,[128] an apology from Prime Minister Harper in the House of Commons, and the creation of two programs, the $24 million Community Historical Recognition Program (CHRP) (for community-based projects) and the $10 million National Historical Recognition Program — NHRP (for federal initiatives).[129] Then Minister of Canadian Heritage Bev Oda was particularly sensitive to historical recognition issues given her Japanese Canadian origin and the impact of the Canadian Japanese Redress Agreement on her community.

Underlying the ACE, CHRP, and NHRP programs were legal and policy analyses that stressed the need to treat the different groups equally. While the situation of Japanese Canadians (loss of property) and Chinese Canadians (payment of the head tax) were different, and provided justification for the symbolic *ex gratia* payments, the commemoration and acknowledgement aspects should treat affected communities equally to avoid possible Charter challenges. ACE provided "initial" funding of $2.5 million to each group.[130] The assumption under CHRP was that at a minimum, the main communities — Chinese Canadian, Italian Canadian, and Ukrainian Canadian — would have equal funding, with some possible "wiggle room" for other affected communities.

Kenney, the Secretary of State at the time, reopened the parameters of CHRP, based on his discussion with the affected communities and his assessment of an appropriate political balance — and of appropriate risk — between the various positions and interests.[131] The end result was:

---

[127] Formally speaking, the Conservative government were accused of reneging on the agreements that had been signed with representatives of the Ukrainian Canadian, Chinese Canadian and Italian Canadian communities, but the "initial amount" of $2.5 million per community was deployed effectively by the affected communities to obtain more funding.

[128] Again, as in the Japanese Canadian model, descendants were not included. Some $16 million in *ex gratia* payments were made to close to 800 persons, the vast majority being spouses of deceased head tax payers.

[129] Prime Minister Harper offers full apology for the Chinese Head Tax, 22 June 2006.

[130] The affected communities understood the $2.5 million to be an initial payment but there was nothing on the official files that committed the Martin government to additional funding.

[131] The difference between the announcement of funding of $34 million and the individual community G&Cs below is accounted for by staff and other costs related to administering the program.

- $10 million as an endowment for the Ukrainian Canadian led World War I Internment Fund, managed by the Ukrainian Canadian Foundation of Taras Shevchenko.[132]

- $5 million each for Chinese Canadian and Italian Canadian projects to be managed by government grants and contributions.

- $2.5 million for Indo-Canadian and Jewish Canadian projects, also to be managed by government grants and contributions, with $400,000 available to other communities.[133]

- A reduction to $5 million for federal initiatives under NHRP, which was essentially directed to the Cave and Basin commemoration of the wartime internment "contribution" of Ukrainian Canadians to the building of Banff National Park.[134]

The Approach

In responding to then Secretary of State Kenney's wish to reopen the 2006 framework for CHRP and NHRP, a number of steps were taken to flag potential risks and issues in 2007 and early 2008 at a number of levels:

Legal Risks

- Throughout the different permutations of historical recognition by various governments, much of the bureaucracy's advice focused on the legal risks involved in treating different groups differently given the Charter. The Japanese Canadian experience was considered to be unique, given the widespread wartime dispersal, expropriation of assets, and returning of Japanese Canadians to Japan. However, the internment experience of Ukrainian Canadians, Italian Canadians, and other affected groups was largely comparable, and immigration restrictions on Indian nationals were arguably similar, broadly speaking, to those on Jewish refugees.

- How could Ukrainian Canadians be granted greater recognition through more funding or a different mechanism (endowment) than Italian Canadians (or German Canadians), when the wartime internment measures, while not identical, were comparable? What was the likelihood of further lawsuits against the government for wartime internment measures, given that there

---

[132] While World War I internment applied to citizens of the Austro-Hungarian Empire, the vast majority were of Ukrainian descent or origin. The endowment agreement was structured to reflect and include other groups affected by these internment measures, although the main focus was on Ukrainian Canadians.

[133] The remaining program funds of some $400,000 were not distributed.

[134] National Historical Recognition Program Update on Parks Canada Projects, Parks Canada, Spring 2010, Volume 1, Issue 1. The portrayal of the internment camps, particularly the balance between the community narrative and the broader national narrative and context, continues to generate some controversy. See Controversy dogs exhibit on First World War internment, The Globe and Mail, 10 June 2013.

was at least one active lawsuit at the time?[135] Were the immigration restrictions against Indo-Canadians hugely different from those against Jewish Canadians? Were there additional program risks in providing differential treatment, in addition to extra complexity?

- There was further advice on the risks of making apologies, either informal apologies, delivered outside Parliament,[136] or more formal ones, delivered in Parliament. At one point, officials tried to parse the various kinds of apologies, the words used (regret, apology, etc.) and the related legal risks. The key language reiterated in legal and policy advice was consistent: "the Head Tax was legal at the time, as acknowledged by Canadian Courts. However, the Government of Canada accepts that the Head Tax was race-based and inconsistent with the values that Canadians hold today."[137] At one time, this language was inserted into press releases (or backgrounders); not surprisingly, it was dropped over time, despite misgivings by officials, as the communities considered it gratuitous. Press releases and speeches were silent on the formal legal disclaimer, and included more conciliatory language:

  > Their experiences mark an unfortunate period in our nation's history. We
  > must ensure that they are never forgotten. ... I am confident that the
  > memorials and the stories shared will not only serve as effective reminders
  > of a difficult time in our history, but also recognize the enormous
  > contributions these communities have made to build Canada.[138]

- In retrospect, while officials had the obligation to provide such advice on the legal and associated policy risks, they may not have sufficiently distinguished between the potential risk and the probability of legal challenges. The political level, acknowledging the theoretical risk flagged by officials (if not always welcoming it), may have had a better sense of the likelihood of this risk being realized, along with their confidence that they could successfully manage the political risks with the various communities. In the end the political level was right, but this was not apparent at the time, given the ongoing Giacomelli case and early signals from some of the communities.

---

[135] The lawsuit concerned Osvaldo Giacomelli, which was originally filed in 2005 and continued by his estate following his death in 2006 (Update from the Estates List - Ontario Bar Association). Because Charter rights expire with the person, his estate's claim was rejected.

[136] The example being then-Prime Minister Mulroney's 1990 apology to Italian Canadians, delivered in a banquet hall.

[137] Example taken from Prime Minister Harper offers full apology for the Chinese Head Tax, 22 June 2006. Subsequent wording changed the reference to the specific measure at issue.

[138] News Release — Minister Kenney marks achievements of the Canadian Historical Recognition Program (CHRP), 18 February 2013 http://www.cic.gc.ca/english/department/media/releases/2013/2013-02-18.asp.

Community Dynamics

- Part of the challenge for officials was understanding the respective strengths, weaknesses, and internal divisions among the various organizations that spoke for each community.[139] While it was never possible to understand the degree to which the concerns of each organization reflected the concerns of each community, officials had to take it as granted that these organizations had political standing and legitimacy. Internal divisions or differences in approach were readily apparent in some organizations, in others less so. Officials were less equipped than those at the political level to appreciate some of these differences and how they might play out (and community organizations had an understandable preference for working with the political level)[140]. Nonetheless, over time, officials developed a better sense of these differences by engaging in key discussions with these organizations.

- Beyond the legal risks discussed above, would the various groups, in particular the Italian Canadian groups, accept being treated differently, with less recognition of their experience? It was clear to officials that the Ukrainian Canadian organizations[141] were more united, well-organized, and had closer relations to the government than the Italian Canadian organizations,[142] and thus the political risk of appearing to favour one community over the other was real. At one point, the Minister's Office correctly noted that while they appreciated officials flagging such political risks, that was more the politicians' responsibility to manage.

---

[139] While it is difficult to know just how well each organization represents community views, for practical reasons the degree to which an organization has standing with the political level tends to be determinant.

[140] On historical recognition files in particular, most of the organizations suspected that officials would be less sympathetic than the political level. They were largely correct, as the political level is intrinsically more open to input from community organizations for legitimate political reasons. Officials, for their part, tend to be more reluctant to acknowledge community claims, given normal bureaucratic reserve and also that the historical record tends to be more complex and more nuanced than sometimes presented by community groups.

For a broader discussion of some of the issues involved in historical recognition, see Margaret MacMillan's *The Uses and Abuses of History* (2008), particularly the "History for Comfort" chapter.

[141] Namely, the Ukrainian Canadian Congress (UCC), the Ukrainian Canadian Civil Liberties Association (UCCLA), and the Ukrainian Canadian Foundation of Taras Shevchenko (UCFTS). It was clear to officials that these organizations enjoyed strong relations with the government, partially reflecting their Western base, and had leeway on a range of issues beyond historical recognition (e.g., recognition of the 1932-3 Holodomor Famine as "an act of genocide," and funding for the Ukrainian Canadian Archives & Museum of Alberta, among others). The Minister spoke at the UCC National Leaders Gala, 6 December 2008, and in his remarks referred to a number of areas where the government was "working on a list" of issues of interest to Ukrainian Canadians.

[142] Namely, the National Congress of Italian Canadians, the Order Sons of Italy of Canada, and the Canadian Italian Professional and Business Association.

This message was reinforced by senior management once these risks had been appropriately raised.[143]

- Officials were included in some of the substantive discussions with the affected communities, in particular with the Ukrainian Canadian, Italian Canadian, and Indo-Canadian communities. Overall, the official role was more technical in nature (what could and could not be done given existing government policies and authorities) since officials had already flagged the major risks of differential treatment.

- Being involved in these discussions helped officials appreciate some of the community politics directly, as well as some of the particular issues facing each community. For example, the insistence by the Ukrainian Canadian community on the government's decision to create an endowment, rather than use government-funded grants and contributions, was driven in part by their wish to have an ongoing source of funding to maintain some historical internment sites (e.g., Spirit Lake Interpretative Centre near Amos, QC),[144] in addition to their preference for direct control over fund disbursements.[145]

- Besides these discussions, ensuring that senior officials attended more community events as well as did relevant background reading (beyond briefing notes) provided a better feel for the dynamics of each community. In this file, as in others, finding the right balance between appearing impartial and objective while developing relationships that improved understanding for both officials and the community organizations remained a challenge.

- Concerning other communities:

  - There were fewer issues and less official-level involvement with the Chinese Canadian community, given that the Chinese Head Tax program was well on its way to providing symbolic *ex gratia* payments totalling close to $16 million to about 800 persons.[146]

---

[143] In the end, our predictions of concern from the Italian Canadian groups that had been active in pushing for historical recognition was correct and led to an opposition private members bill, C-302 (*Italian Canadian Recognition and Restitution Act*) in 2010. The government opposed it. Officials, as is normal, had to provide input to the government speeches opposing the bill. See MPs vote for apology to Italian-Canadians, but Tories opposed, *The Toronto Star*, 28 April 2010, and *Hansard*, 30 March 2010 for Dean del Mastro, then Parliamentary Secretary to the Minister of Canadian Heritage. The bill had a number of drafting flaws that would have exposed the government to potential liability for individual claims; in the end, the bill progressed to the Senate where the Government effectively delayed consideration until the 40th Session of Parliament ended with the election of 2011.

[144] Launch of Quebec Internment Spirit Lake Interpretive Centre, La Ferme, Quebec, 19 August 2010.

[145] This was made clear in a meeting in the fall of 2007 between the Minister, his staff, and officials with the three Ukrainian Canadian organizations.

[146] Some organizations, like the Chinese Canadian National Council (CCNC), still maintained their position in favor of *ex gratia* payments for descendants (Head Tax Redress Campaign), creating some difficulties and tensions once funds started flowing for community projects under CHRP. The National Congress of Chinese Canadians (NCCC) was more supportive.

- Similarly, the Jewish Canadian community raised no major concerns that officials were aware of, partly because the Minister's Office deftly ensured that the major organizations each had a high visibility flagship project.[147] Other files of interest to the community also helped: Canada becoming a member of the International Holocaust Remembrance Alliance, an active role by the Minister in the Inter-Parliamentary Coalition to Combat Antisemitism and related conferences, Public Safety's *Communities at Risk: Security Infrastructure* Program, and the government's shift towards greater support of Israel.

- Officials were more involved in discussions with the Indo-Canadian community, helping with earlier public consultations by then MP Jim Abbott in 2007 and subsequent meetings.[148] The main issues were internal to the community, concerning more the nature of recognition rather than the level of funding. For example, a wide range of opinions were collected on what would constitute appropriate recognition for the Komagata Maru, and related immigration restrictions, including the question of an apology.[149]

- In addition to being involved in meetings and discussions with the various groups to understand better the depth of their concerns, I found it particularly helpful to read some of the "classics" on some of the internment measures or immigration restrictions to give me the broader context and narrative. Particularly helpful were Joy Kogawa's *Obasan* on Japanese Canadian internment (literature can be more powerful than academic texts!), Irving Abella and Harold Troper's *None is Too Many: Canada and the Jews of Europe 1933-48*, and Hugh Johnston's *The Voyage of the Komagata Maru: The Sikh Challenge to Canada's Colour Bar*.

World War I Internment Fund

- Given the Ukrainian Canadian community's wish for an endowment, officials needed to carry out due diligence on the capacity and risks related to the proposed vehicle to manage the endowment, The Ukrainian Canadian Foundation of Taras Shevchenko. As the Foundation had a history of managing its existing endowment of some $7 million[150] with the necessary policies, process, and financial statements in place, this was feasible from a program risk

---

[147] B'nai Brith held a symposium in 2009, *The St. Louis Era: Looking Back, Moving Forward*, as part of Canada's membership bid for the International Holocaust Remembrance Alliance. The Canadian Jewish Congress (now merged into The Centre for Israel and Jewish Affairs) led the building of The Wheel of Conscience monument at The Canadian Museum of Immigration at Pier 21, Halifax, inaugurated in 2011.

[148] See the Report of Meetings with Representatives of the Indo–Canadian Community.

[149] Prime Minister Harper made an apology at an Indo-Canadian community picnic on 3 August 2008. It was a "drive-by" apology, to use the irreverent words of officials, and received mixed reviews from the Indo-Canadian community as it was not delivered in Parliament. See Harper apologizes in B.C. for 1914 Komagata Maru incident, *CBC*, 3 August 2008.

[150] In March 2012, their annual report showed some $3.5 million in the Foundation endowment and some $8.8 million in managed funds.

perspective. Nonetheless, getting clarity from Treasury Board Secretariat and the Finance Branch at Canadian Heritage took time and effort; new endowments were rare.

- Interestingly, the model chosen for the endowment fund was different from that used for the Japanese Canadian endowment to establish the Canadian Race Relations Foundation (CRRF). The Japanese Canadian community wanted the CRRF to be closely connected to government, as an arms-length Crown corporation with Board members appointed directly by the government. The Ukrainian Canadian community insisted on autonomy and control; officials never provided any advice on alternate models, including the CRRF model, given that the policy direction was set and the government was comfortable with granting the community autonomy.[151]

- An endowment agreement required a formal agreement for the new entity: the Canadian First World War Internment Recognition Fund. While much of the agreement was fairly standard boilerplate accountability, reporting, and other provisions, there were a number of issues that required care:

  - The endowment was to provide for projects that covered all affected communities, not just Ukrainian Canadians;

  - Governance, particularly the Endowment Council, was to ensure balanced representation between the three Ukrainian Canadian organizations, three representatives from other affected communities, and a neutral Chair. While the Ukrainian Canadian organizations wanted a fourth spot to represent the descendants of internees, officials recommended against having majority Ukrainian Canadian representation. In the end, an observer position, left vague, was allowed;[152]

  - Ensuring that the agreement stipulated projects should Canadian-based, to avoid the temptation of some for international travel; and,

  - To preserve the capital of the endowment. Only the income from the $10 million could be spent for program and administrative expenses for the first 15 years of the Fund.

- Ironically, and unfortunately, the $10 million was transferred shortly after the announcement on 9 May 2008, and was promptly invested in what was considered a prudent mix of equities and bonds before the crash of fall 2008, leading to a loss of approximately $1 million which the

---

[151] There are advantages and disadvantages to each approach. It is unclear whether the CRRF has met the original objectives envisaged by the Japanese Canadian community, and the increased overhead of being a Crown corporation is costly. A long-term comparison of the CRRF with the WWI Internment Fund would shed some light on the benefits and disadvantages of each model.

[152] Internal community politics made this a difficult issue for the Ukrainian Canadian organizations. This was one of the last issues resolved, and required confirmation of the Minister's Office to hold firm on the Ukrainian Canadian community having only three out of seven representatives. The MO did hold firm, recognizing the importance of balanced representation, both substantively and from an optics point of view. Program and political risks were aligned.

Fund has since recovered. Since its inception, the Fund has disbursed $728,000, with further commitments of $555,000 through to 2015.[153]

Other Endowment Requests

- Given the Italian Canadian groups' desire for an endowment, officials requested documents and other evidence proving that they had previous experience handling endowments. The groups provided copies of their financial statements but had no equivalent to the Taras Shevchenko Foundation. As a result, officials could not recommend an endowment approach. The political level accepted their judgment. Unfortunately, due to a mix-up in communications between officials and the Minister's Office, this analysis had not been shared with the Minister prior to a conference call in 2008 with the representatives of the Italian Canadian organizations, which, needless to say, turned out to be an awkward meeting.[154]

- In the end, given the difficulties in coming to terms with the Italian Canadian organizations, the government proceeded with the announcement of the new CHRP including only the Chinese Canadian, Ukrainian Canadian and Indo-Canadian communities in May 2008.

- As an endowment was not feasible from a program perspective for the Italian Canadians, and because these organizations were insistent on comparable treatment to the Ukrainian Canadian community, officials had a limited role as this issue played itself out at the political level. In the end, the Italian Canadian groups overplayed their hand and the government chose an alternative approach, appointing a Conservative Senator of Italian origin, Consiglio Di Nino, to help manage the politics and put in place an advisory committee that would have credibility within the broader Italian Canadian community.[155]

Program Risks

Once the framework of CHRP and NHRP had been decided, the normal implementation of program design took place. The following program risks were taken into account:

---

[153] Canadian First World War Internment Recognition Fund Annual Report 2012.

[154] Lesson learned for both Ministerial staff and officials to ensure better preparation for such calls. Nothing can be more awkward than having a Minister turn to an official, expecting a certain course of action, and the official having to outline issues that made that course of action difficult if not impossible to achieve.

[155] His efforts were successful, and the government announced an advisory committee on 19 March 2009. See Government of Canada announces Italian Canadian Advisory Committee members for historical recognition projects, with the members being Palmacchio (Pal) Di Iulio as chair, Roberto Perin as vice-chair and Joe Papa, none of them affiliated with the Italian Canadian organizations that had been pressing for historical recognition. Professor Roberto Perrin is the co-author of Enemies Within: Italian and Other Internees in Canada and Abroad, which placed the Italian Canadian wartime experience in the context of some fascistic tendencies within the community during that period. A further irony: the fact that relatively few project ideas emerged from the Italian Canadian community, and officials were tasked with outreach in 2010 to help generate more projects.

- The normal accountability provisions had to ensure value for money and appropriate financial accountability;

- Everyone struggled to find the right balance between community initiative and official-level support to meet the normal requirements of government grants and contributions programs. Due to the nature of many of the proposed projects, and the inexperience of many of these community organizations in meeting the complex documentation requirements of the program, staff spent considerable time and effort guiding and supporting them through the application process;

- Creating credible advisory committees by suggesting names, or commenting on names suggested by the Minister's Office, helped to ensure that the community's different interests were well represented. Not surprisingly, the Minister's Office had a better feel than officials for some of these issues and community dynamics (sometimes more subjective than objective), but officials were still able to contribute to these discussions.

- Officials welcomed advisory committees even if there were challenges with some of the internal dynamics, largely because any recommended project was likely to be approved by the Minister, in sharp contrast to the higher rejection rate of multiculturalism projects developed by officials. In a sense, this reduced program risk considerably. Any project recommended up the line would not be rejected at the last instance.

- The transfer to CIC, and CIC Finance's unfamiliarity with smaller organizations and grants and contributions projects, resulted in considerable time and effort being put into managing, at the bureaucratic level, perceived risk. From a program perspective, Finance focused too much on potential risk, without taking into account the value of projects (some as small as $50,000), or fixated excessively on financial statements without taking into account the track record of the organization and the community in delivering similar projects.[156]

While the overall parameters and direction were driven by the political level, the process of historical recognition reflected a high degree of collaboration with officials in the detailed program design. The government was successful in delivering a program that largely satisfied the demands of most communities. Projects large and small told the stories of internment and immigration restrictions. The officials' caution was well placed but lacking. Officials needed the insight of the political level in coming up with the final package that translated the formal "equal treatment" approach into one that took into account the different historical experiences and respective political factors of each community.

---

[156] The most ludicrous example was the fixation on financial statements for the MS St. Louis monument (designed by Daniel Libeskind and developed by the Canadian Jewish Congress), commemorating the Canadian government's refusal of some 900 Jewish Refugees, which demonstrated a lack of any understanding of the capacity and commitment of the Jewish Canadian community. Common sense prevailed in the end, but at one point officials had to send press clippings to demonstrate progress (e.g., Daniel Libeskind memorial to mark Canada's refusal of Jews in 1939, *The Globe and Mail*, 30 August 2010).

Chapter 5

Some Gaps and Omissions

This chapter covers issues that received less attention from the Minister because of political considerations and sensitivities. In contrast to some of the core citizenship and multiculturalism issues covered earlier, which were driven by the political level, there was little political pull when it came to developing a better understanding of Quebec's model of multiculturalism, *interculturalisme*, and issues related to radicalization and social cohesion. Nevertheless, officials continued policy work as these issues were related to recurring themes in Canadian media and political discourse, and were linked to some of the key principles underlying citizenship and multiculturalism.

As there was extensive work on policies, programs, and delivery methods on citizenship, the main gaps pertained to multiculturalism. The government's clear political direction towards more meaningful — read restrictive — citizenship meant that there was little appetite or capacity for more open-ended policy work on citizenship in a global, interdependent world, although one internal paper was prepared to capture the history related to citizenship policy.[157]

QUEBEC DEBATES AND *INTERCULTURALISME*

Understandably, given political sensitivities, the Minister and government largely stayed on the sidelines of the ongoing Quebec debates over multiculturalism, *interculturalisme*, integration, and diversity.

Interculturalisme and *interculturalité* were developed by the <u>Ordre des traducteurs, terminologues et interprètes agréés du Québec</u> to reflect Quebec's "distinct" interpretation of Canada's multiculturalism ethos. The idea was to insist that newcomers should aspire to integrate themselves into Quebec national and cultural identity, not the more amorphous pan-Canadian identity.

Quebec's model of diversity, *interculturalisme*, was increasingly positioned as being in opposition to Canadian multiculturalism, rather than as a variant or complement of it. Within Quebec there lies a prevalent mythology that Canadian multiculturalism was implemented by former Prime Minister Trudeau to diminish Quebec and Francophone Canada by rejecting biculturalism. While it is true that Trudeau rejected biculturalism and nationalism in favor of a focus on individual rights, both in the broader and language rights contexts, the prevailing myth

---

[157] In early 2008, there was a "citizenship futures" discussion deck that laid out some general options and scenarios for citizenship policy, suggesting that the current balance was largely appropriate. Following Minister Kenney's arrival at CIC, the current direction towards more meaningful citizenship was set.

meant that many Quebecers perceived multiculturalism policy as a diminishment of French Canadians from founding culture to just another ethnic community:

> C'est exactement ce que souhaitait faire Pierre Trudeau en 1971, quand il a fait voter la Loi sur le multiculturalisme canadien, dont le but premier était de banaliser le statut de la culture québécoise au Canada. Le couronnement de cette opération est venu en 1982, lorsque la Charte des droits a été enchâssée dans la Constitution, avec ses dispositions renforçant le multiculturalisme. Au fil des années, la Charte canadienne a permis une attaque sournoise contre deux valeurs fondamentales dans l'identité du Québec moderne: le fait français et la laïcité.[158]

This was not the first federal approach to be so characterized, but it was particularly ignorant of the role that Canadians of origins other than Aboriginal, French, and English played in the development of the multiculturalism policy. In particular, Ukrainian Canadians viewed their

---

[158] See Frédéric Bastien, Diversité culturelle - De Trudeau à Charest, même combat, *Le Devoir*, 10 October 2009. Informal translation:

> This is exactly what Pierre Trudeau was hoping to do in 1971when the Canadian Multiculturalism Act was voted into law. The first goal of this law was to trivialize the status of Quebecois culture in Canada. The pinnacle of this act came in 1982 when the Charter of Rights was entrenched in the Constitution, with provisions reinforcing multiculturalism. Over the years, the Canadian Charter allowed for an underhanded attack on two fundamental values in Quebec's modern identity: the French fact and secularism.

Also Louise Beaudoin, then PQ porte-parole de l'opposition officielle en matière de Relations internationales et de Francophonie, de Laïcité et de Condition feminine, who, in responding to security staff at the Assembleé nationale stopping Sikh-Canadians from testifying, stated in an opinion piece, Libre opinion - Le Québec et le multiculturalisme, *Le Devoir*, 15 February 2011:

> Je le renvoie aux travaux du politicologue canadien Kenneth McRoberts qui a bien démontré que Trudeau a utilisé ce concept pour mieux rejeter celui des «deux nations», qu'il abhorrait. C'est le refus de reconnaître l'existence de cette nation qui l'a conduit à vouloir diluer son existence dans un ensemble plus vaste, avec les effets pervers que reconnaissent maintenant beaucoup de Canadiens anglais, à gauche comme à droite.

Informal translation:

> I refer him to the work of Canadian political analyst Kenneth McRoberts, who clearly demonstrated that Trudeau used this concept to better reject the idea of "two nations", which he detested. It was his refusal to recognize the existence of this nation that led him to want to dilute its existence as part of a greater whole, with the negative effects that many English Canadians recognize today, whether they be liberal or conservative.

contribution to the settling and development of the West as similar to that of French and British settlers elsewhere in Canada.[159]

At the official level, while Canadian Heritage had an active and ongoing interest in Quebec files and debates, CIC did not, as immigrant selection and integration/settlement had been devolved to Quebec under the 1978 Cullen-Couture Agreement. Prior to the arrival of the Multiculturalism Program, the citizenship program was the main touch point between CIC and citizens in Quebec. Rather than seeing the citizenship program as an opportunity to enhance federal presence, the government largely managed it from a narrow program delivery perspective.[160]

This lack of attention was prudent at the political level: Quebec engaged in an European-like debate, suspicious and unwelcoming of newcomers. To help manage this debate and the related politics, the Charest government created the Bouchard-Taylor Commission in 2007 to conduct hearings on diversity and accommodation-related issues across Quebec. The resulting 2008 report, *Fonder l'avenir: Le temps de la conciliation*, was intellectually sound, innovative, and thoughtful, both in the general and Quebec-specific senses. However, the report's recommendations were ultimately unsuccessful, as they were not implemented. The Commission, Report, and related follow-up debates passed largely without federal government comment, although officials followed the deliberations and debates closely.[161]

The federal government also stayed mostly silent on the wide range of Quebec accommodation issues during this period.[162] The 2007 Hérouxville Code of Conduct on Quebec Values provided a focal point for much of the debate in Quebec, and was taken up by the official opposition in the Quebec Assemblée nationale at the time.[163]

---

[159] See Manoly R. Lupul, *The Politics of Multiculturalism: A Ukrainian Canadian Memoir* (Edmonton: Canadian Institute of Ukrainian Studies Press, 2005) and Daniel Jesse Westlake, *Building multiculturalism : the contribution of the Ukrainian Canadian Community to a re-thinking of Canadian identity*, Master's Thesis, 2010.

[160] An example of this was the large-scale citizenship ceremonies in Montreal (between 200-300 new citizens at a time) which, while efficient, may have been less effective than the smaller, more intimate ceremonies practiced elsewhere in Canada.

[161] Only Josée Verner, then-Minister of Intergovernmental Affairs, voiced her support for a proposed charter on laïcité, which would give priority to women's rights. See A rights debate gone wrong, *The Globe and Mail*, 16 October 2009.

[162] See Section II of the Bouchard-Taylor Report for the details of most of these incidents, and its setting of the facts behind the media "frenzy." The chronic insensitivity to accommodation continues, the most recent incident being the decision by the Fédération de soccer du Québec to ban Sikh players wearing turbans. See Lettre ouverte à la Fédération de soccer du Québec: Le Foot pour tous!, *Le Devoir*, 8 June 2013, and for more reasonable commentary, Soccer - Le turban ravive les tensions entre Québec et Ottawa, *Le Devoir*, 12 June 2013, which explains how this reflects internal Quebec and federal-provincial politics.

[163] For the Hérouxville Code of Conduct, see http://municipalite.herouxville.qc.ca/normes.pdf.

POLICY ARROGANCE OR INNOCENT BIAS

In the lead-up to the 2008 federal election, the Bloc Québecois tabled Bill C-505 (*An Act to amend the Canadian Multiculturalism Act (non-application in Quebec)*).[164] Needless to say, the government could not stay silent, and Minister Kenney was particularly — and typically — forceful:

> They seem very keen on trying to find symbolic issues and to use those to send what some people call dog whistle messages — messages that can be interpreted different ways by different audiences. I think maybe in a certain sense they are sending a dog whistle message to some that they are against the growing ethnocultural diversity in Greater Montreal in particular and in Quebec in general.[165]

But it was the ongoing issue of accommodation in relation to the niqab where federal messaging was initially mixed. At the purely federal level, the Prime Minister publicly criticized the Chief Electoral Officer for not banning the niqab during voting, even though Election Canada's enabling legislation required it to provide options for electors with face coverings in 2007.[166]

In Quebec, the 2010 case of a niqab-wearing student who was expelled from French-language settlement classes after her demands for accommodation were considered disruptive to other students attracted widespread attention across Canada.[167] Soon after, the Charest government introduced Bill C-94 (*Une acte établissant des balises encadrant les demandes d'accommodement dans l'administration publique et dans certains établissements*), banning individuals from wearing the niqab when receiving public services. Intergovernmental Affairs Minister Josée Verner supported the

---

[164] The Bill was extremely concise:
> 1. The preamble of the Canadian Multiculturalism Act is amended by adding the following after the seventh paragraph:

> AND WHEREAS Quebeckers form a nation and must therefore possess all the tools needed to define their identity and protect their common values, particularly as regards the protection of the French language, the separation of church and state, and gender equality;

> 2. Section 3 of the Act is amended by adding the following after subsection (2):

> (3) The Government of Canada's multiculturalism policy does not apply in Quebec.

[165] BQ desperate, Tory minister says, *The Gazette*, 17 September 2008. Official input to speeches used more neutral language:
> With that in mind, special attention is paid to the economic, social and cultural integration of new Canadians. We all know that these three areas are essential for a feeling of belonging to develop and thrive. (Conservative MP Denis Lebel, Roberval - Lac St.-Jean, 16 June 2008).

[166] See 6 niqab legal controversies in Canada, *CBC*, 20 December 2012.

[167] See Une musulmane expulsée d'un cours à cause du niqab, *Cyberpresse*, 2 March 2010.

move, while Minister Kenney, through a spokesperson, reaffirmed Quebec's jurisdiction.[168] Yet a few weeks later, when asked about CIC's procedures regarding women wearing the niqab, Minister Kenney stated a classic accommodation position, likely reflecting his views on religious freedom:[169]

> He instead confirmed that it was not a question of telling people how to dress, except when proper identification is needed. "In my department, when a woman arrives wearing a face covering, as part of an application for immigration or a visa, we insist that she show her face. ... In these cases, generally, officials provide a female official to interact with the individual as often as possible."[170]

In 2011 policy changed when the Minister announced that the niqab would not be allowed at citizenship ceremonies, given the inability of citizenship judges to see if potential citizen was speaking — or at least mouthing — the words when swearing the citizenship oath. Accommodation was no longer allowed. Kenney aligned himself to the Quebec approach — and Canadian public opinion.[171] He stated the reasons in value terms:

> It's a "public declaration that you are joining the Canadian family and it must be taken freely and openly," [Kenney] said, calling it "frankly, bizarre" that women were allowed to wear face veils while they swear their citizenship oaths.

> Kenney said he doesn't accept that it's a religious obligation to wear the veil, explaining that when Muslim women perform the hajj, the pilgrimage to Mecca required by their faith, they are required not to cover their faces.

> "It's a cultural tradition, which I think reflects a certain view about women that we don't accept in Canada. We want women to be full and equal

---

[168] Feds offer limited support to Quebec in niqab uproar, *Montreal Gazette*, 5 March 2010.

[169] The original "house card" said nothing until it was pointed out that the Minister might be asked about how his department handles niqab-wearing women.

[170] Le niqab des solitudes, *Le Devoir*, 20 March 2010.

[171] According to a 2010 Angus-Reid poll, 80 percent of Canadians outside of Quebec supported the Quebec niqab legislation (Most Canadians Support Quebecs Veil Ban, *Angus Reid*, 29 March 2010). It's likely that a similar number would support the ban on the niqab at citizenship ceremonies. A contrary, and thoughtful, view from Professor Clifford Orwin notes that Canadian democracy and multiculturalism is a large tent and a broad-minded one (No room at the inn for veiled women? Get real, Canada, *The Globe and Mail*, 23 August 2012). A more conventional view, also thoughtful, can be found in Dan Gardner's The canvas of emotion, *The Ottawa Citizen*, 14 December 2011.

members of Canadian society and certainly when they're taking the citizenship oath, that's the right place to start."[172]

While the political level largely minimized its interventions in Quebec discussions and rarely used official-level input in its few public statements, officials followed Quebec debates closely — both the helpful ones (the Bouchard-Taylor report) and the less so (the periodic media eruptions). Underlying this was the need for a better understanding of the similarities and differences between Quebec's *interculturalisme* and Canadian multiculturalism models.

As sometimes happens, opportunities emerge by chance. I happened to encounter Gérard Bouchard at a Canadian studies conference at Oxford in 2009, where we were both presenting. He noted, as one of the few readers of the *Annual Report on the Canadian Multiculturalism Act*, how much Minister Kenney had shifted the emphasis to integration, and how the Quebec and Canadian models were closer as a result. Subsequently, he contacted CIC requesting financial support for an international symposium on *interculturalisme* he was organizing in May 2011.[173] CIC was only too happy to provide some funding, and this allowed some long-overdue comparative analysis on the two respective models to take place.

Over the space of a few months leading up to the Symposium, the department shared drafts with Professor Bouchard and his colleagues to help improve federal understanding of the Bouchard model of *interculturalisme* (or, to crib a concept from the Bouchard-Taylor report, *interculturalisme ouvert*), and his efforts to develop a model that addressed the sensitivities of the Quebec Francophone population, a minority in anglophone North America:

> In dual societies, therefore (or more precisely: in societies where ethnoculturality is addressed through the lens of a duality), a balance must be struck between the perpetuation and development of majority cultures, taking into account their ongoing history and founding myths, and the integration of minorities, taking into account their rights. The main challenge is to arbitrate between majorities and minorities in a spirit of conciliation, interaction and negotiation that respects ethnocultural diversity, while providing for the continuing cultural identity of founding groups and their heritage. Respect for the fundamental values of host societies and the emergence of shared cultural expressions and practices,

---

[172] Face veils banned for citizenship oaths, *CBC*, 12 December 2011. Interestingly, Kenney's pronouncement on the niqab not being a requirement of Islam, while correct, marks a different approach to Supreme Court jurisprudence which generally takes personal religious beliefs as given, rather than questioning particular interpretations or beliefs.

[173] Interculturalisme 2011 - International Symposium on Interculturalism. Part of the challenge of paradigms like dual societies is that few societies are so monolithic as to posit such a duality. Quebec also includes a historical aboriginal element, for example, a fact that highlights the need for nuance.

as part of the process of integration, also are at the heart of interculturalism. [174]

The result was a series of tables that compared multiculturalism and *interculturalisme* that, while not fully reconciling the two models, revealed greater commonality between the two (particularly given the federal government's more explicit emphasis on the integrative aspects of multiculturalism) than most political, academic, and media commentary.

The first table captures the high-level paradigms of the various diversity models:

Table 9: Diversity Paradigms[175]

Paradigm	Characteristics	Examples
Diversity	Individuals and groups equal and protected by same rights, no formal recognition of majority or minorities	US, Sweden, Australia, India, English Canada
Unitary	No official ethnocultural differentiation in public life	France, Japan, Russia
Multi-Polarity	Societies officially constituted of groups and subgroups	Malaysia, Bolivia, Belgium, Switzerland, Northern Ireland, Canada
Layered Duality	Relationship between a) ethnocultural minorities and recent immigrants, and b) an ethnocultural (founding) majority, that is a minority within a majority	Quebec

The second table then looks at these high level paradigms and applies them to a contrast between multiculturalism and *interculturalisme*:

---

[174] Steering Paper, International Symposium on Interculturalism, May 2011.

[175] Working Document, winter 2011, updated 2013.

Table 10: Multiculturalism/Interculturalisme Comparison[176]

Element	Interculturalisme	Multiculturalism
Identity	Nation Québecois and aboriginal	Aboriginal, bilingual and diverse
Context	Minority within national (and continental) majority	National framework, regional application
Majority culture	Officially recognized and promoted	Implicit and assumed, but increased promotion and awareness of Canadian identity
Emphasis	Focus on interaction, bringing together, feeling of belonging and integration	Integration and accommodation dynamic, recent focus on commonalities
Language	Protection and promotion of French	Two official languages, English dominant language in North America
Values	Slightly more explicit formulation along Francophone lines	More case by case but within general societal and Charter values
Collective memory	Strong shared collective memory and narrative	Integration and accommodation dynamic within context of history, identity, and values

The lack of activity of CIC's Policy Committee (2011) and the departure of key officials involved meant that this collaboration and analysis was abandoned. As for the federal official-level participation at the *Interculturalisme* Symposium, a safe boilerplate presentation was used. The federal government missed an opportunity to counter some of the myths behind *interculturalisme* versus multiculturalism.[177]

RADICALIZATION AND SOCIAL COHESION

After the 9/11 World Trade Centre attacks, the British 2005 London bombings, and a range of other terrorist attacks in a number of countries, Western governments paid more and more attention to domestic and international terrorist threats. The bulk of these efforts, appropriately enough, took place on the security side of government. But most governments, the UK being most ambitious with its "Prevent" strategy following the London attacks, placed considerable

---

[176] Working Document, winter 2011, updated 2013.

[177] Le pari moderne et civique du multiculturalisme canadien, presentation delivered 27 May 2011.

emphasis on the social side, attempting to find ways to prevent their citizens and residents from becoming radicalized.

Radicalization and social cohesion were issues of interest to the Canadian government. The Departments of Public Safety and Justice created the Cross-Cultural Roundtable on Security (CCRS) in 2005 to provide a consultative forum with representatives from a variety of communities.[178] While the focus of most of the meetings was consultation on specific policy and program initiatives, the CCRS provided a useful focus for more general policy discussions and understanding of the factors and approaches in dealing with radicalization from a social policy perspective. In the days of Canadian Heritage, officials of the Multiculturalism Program were regular participants at meetings of the CCRS; after the move to CIC, Multiculturalism Program participation diminished and was largely replaced by CIC's Strategic Policy group. However, the Multiculturalism Program continued to use, as needed, the CCRS as one of its consultation fora.

The CCRS was particularly active on understanding the dynamics and approaches related to radicalization in 2008, which helped inform the approach of the Multiculturalism Program. In particular, the Program consulted CCRS members in March on a proposed approach, noting the shift of the Multiculturalism Program towards integration and a focus on Canadian identity and values, and asking members about their views on two open-ended questions:

1. What is the appropriate role for Canadian Heritage and its Multicultural Program in countering radicalization?

2. Are traditional government objectives (civic participation, antiracism/cross-cultural understanding, inclusive institutions) enough to address radicalization, or are radicalization-specific initiatives required? [179]

Concurrently, through the development of new priorities for multiculturalism grants and contributions projects mentioned in Chapter 2, Minister Kenney was signaling an early interest in supporting projects that aimed at reducing radicalization and improving social cohesion. As noted, the third priority that emerged in 2008 made an explicit reference to radicalization:

- Promoting intercultural understanding and Canadian values (democracy, freedom, human rights, and rule of law) through community initiatives, with the objective of addressing issues of cultural social exclusion (parallel communities) and radicalization.[180]

---

[178] Cross-Cultural Roundtable on Security, Public Safety Website.

[179] Heritage department takes aim at religious radicals, *The Globe and Mail*, 1 September 2008.

[180] *The Way Forward*, Annual Report on the Operation of the Canadian Multiculturalism Act 2007-2008.

In subsequent years, a number of projects were funded that were aligned, more or less closely, with the aim of reducing the potential for radicalization, as indicated in the table below:[181]

Table 11: Radicalization-Related Multiculturalism Projects

Community	Organization	Project and Funding Amount	Objectives
Muslim (Youth)	Canadian Council of Muslim Women	MY CANADA (2009-2011, $471k)	Understanding of rule of law, Canadian identity, dealing with local challenges and how to prevent radicalization.
Somali	Canadian International Peace Project	Somali / Jewish Canadian Mentorship Project (2009-2011, $474k)	Long-term community cohesion and cadre of young Somali Canadian professionals able to assume leadership roles and contribute to Canadian society.
Somali	Canadian Friends of Somalia	Promoting Peace and Preventing Youth Radicalization (2010, $15k)	Develop a better understanding of challenges facing Somali youth. Topics include radicalization of Somali youth in the West and underlying causes of youth radicalization, countering youth radicalization and best practices in deradicalization, and building an integrated and socially responsible Somali diaspora.
Somali	Somali Canadian Cultural Society of Edmonton	Reducing Barriers for Somali at Risk Youth within their Community and School System (2009-2012, $166k)	Gain awareness, knowledge and skills for civic engagement; identify and take action toward resolving issues affecting their communities; and wider participation in civil society.
South Asian (Sinhalese, Tamil, etc.)	The Mosaic Institute for Harnessing Diversity	South-Asian Global Citizenship Project (2009-2011, $150k)	Participant engagement in community service projects supporting ethnocultural groups beyond their own communities. Sharing this model with other communities and cross-cultural bridging initiatives.
Youth	Canadian Centre for Diversity	Diversity is Youth Peer Leaders (2009-2013, $1.2M)	Build a network of skilled and trained young leaders focused on preventing and responding to conflicts; provide a community of support within to reinforce social cohesion and inclusion, while strengthening community.
Youth (ethnocultural)	Leave out ViolencE, British Columbia	The Prism Project (2009-2012, $180k)	Reduce violence in the lives of youth; youth find meaningful employment and complete high school; increased awareness of violence associated with culture and race.
Youth (Indo-Canadian)	Surrey School District, British Columbia	Surrey Appreciates Multi-Ethnicity (2009-2010, $895k)	Develop knowledge, self-confidence, cultural pride, leadership, and decision-making skills needed for cross-cultural relationships. Build bridges and social cohesion among diverse ethnocultural communities.

---

[181] Working draft, Annex to Memo to the Minister, Update on Radicalization Work, winter 2011. One of the favourites of the Minister, cited often in his speeches, was the Somali-Jewish Mentorship Project. While couched in terms of improving cross-cultural understanding and inclusion, implicitly it aimed at reducing potential radicalization and gang involvement. See Minister Kenney announces support for innovative mentorship project, 12 June 2009.

As noted earlier, with the transfer to CIC, policy development required greater intra-departmental consultation, in addition to the ongoing consultations and collaboration with Public Safety. Somewhat ironically, discussions with Public Safety were, in many ways, easier, as Public Safety officials had a better understanding of the issues and, given their exchanges with other countries, had an appreciation of the role that social policy and programs could play, even if only at the margins.

Among both multiculturalism officials and the broader CIC community, there was considerable debate on how to frame and define radicalization. Part of this was legitimate, but it also reflected the time-honoured bureaucratic technique of taking refuge in definitions to avoid thinking about and discussion of the harder issues. Two main tendencies emerged:

1. Focusing only on violent extremism or radicalization, largely the purview of security agencies, while supporting projects and policies that had a range of social cohesion aims;

2. Taking a broader approach to radicalization, not limited to violent extremism, acknowledging the challenges that non-violent radicalization can bring to integration and social cohesion, and where there may be a broader social policy role.

The latter approach, while more closely aligned with the Minister, created unease among officials who were concerned that such a broad definition of what constituted radicalization meant also singling out legitimate political discourse and dissent.[182] After all, in a democratic society, freedom of speech, freedom of religion, freedom of conscience, and the general human rights framework all imply openness and tolerance of those minorities who chose to live out their understanding of their religious and cultural practices (provided, of course, that these do not conflict with Canadian laws and the rights of others).

The counter argument was that while individuals had the right to live their lives according to their religious and cultural beliefs (with the caveat above), the potential impact on social cohesion was significant if more and more individuals and communities chose to live apart and not participate in the wider community. Finding a balance between respecting individual minority rights while still encouraging broader participation and social cohesion was a challenge, but the potential for individuals and communities to turn inward, and not be part of the wider community, could not be ignored — even if it did not involve violent radicalization or extremism.

At the level of Policy Committee these issues were never fully resolved. Nonetheless, Executive Committee provided clearer direction: consult with affected and other communities to validate and refine the proposed approach, and support and contribute to a "whole of government" strategy on radicalization. As part of this process, a number of fora were particularly helpful:

---

[182] Amusingly, part of the problem was the term radicalization. Many people around the table in Policy Committee thought back to their youth, sometimes through rose-tinted glasses, considering radicalization in a more liberalizing context than the radicalization of more conservative interpretations of religion.

POLICY ARROGANCE OR INNOCENT BIAS

- While the Multiculturalism Program was a junior partner with Public Safety, much of Public Safety's research and policy work was helpful in validating the social policy and program role as a complement to the work of security agencies.

- Tracking the experience of other jurisdictions, particularly the UK but also other countries such as Australia, Denmark, and the Netherlands, gave a sense of what worked and what did not (while still recognizing that the context in each country was different). Much of this information came from Public Safety, directly or through CCRS discussions, besides participation at various Metropolis conferences, an Integration Working Group of the Intergovernmental Consultations on Migration, Asylum and Refugees (IGC) and bilateral meetings. The key message that emerged, particularly but not exclusively from the UK, was the need to keep security and "community resilience" initiatives separate. Otherwise, efforts to strengthen community resilience would become suspect and less effective.[183]

- Domestic consultations, albeit with the involvement of fewer communities than desired, in October 2010.[184] Key messages that emerged were:

  - Agreement that a social cohesion approach, similar to that in the above projects, and focused on enhancing intercultural and interfaith understanding, would be beneficial;

  - Need to understand the particular dynamics and issues of each community, and target strategies to address these particular dynamics and issues. One size does not fit all;

  - A number of risks were identified:

    - Feeling, on the part of communities, of being targeted;

    - Portraying issue as one between newcomer/immigrant communities;

    - Reducing the credibility of program partners if they are perceived to be a voice of government;

    - Supporting organizations that do not represent or fully engage women and youth, with attendant consequences; and,

---

[183] From the UK evaluation of the PREVENT initiative: Prevent review, June 2011:

> The *Prevent* programme we inherited from the last Government was flawed. It confused the delivery of Government policy to promote integration with Government policy to prevent terrorism. It failed to confront the extremist ideology at the heart of the threat we face; and in trying to reach those at risk of radicalisation, funding sometimes even reached the very extremist organisations that *Prevent* should have been confronting.

[184] Unfortunately, while efforts were made to have as broad a representation of communities affected by radicalization or extremism as possible, a number of last minute cancellations meant that Muslim Canadians were disproportionately represented. The diversity among Muslim Canadians present made, however, for a lively and helpful discussion.

- Indirectly contributing to radicalization by funding intolerant groups that do not reflect Canadian values.[185]

These observations were subsequently discussed with the CCRS the following month. All parties broadly agreed; CCRS members also stressed the importance of programming that engaged women and youth.[186]

- Participation in Public Safety organized the bilateral Canada-United States Joint Working Session with representatives from the Department of Homeland Security (DHS) starting in fall 2010. The item of particular relevance to the Multiculturalism Program was: "Exchange research, information, and best practices on programs and initiatives aimed at promoting resilient communities, including community outreach/engagement, and integration-based programming."

One of the constraining factors for officials was the government's sensitivity when talking to certain individuals and groups, primarily those from the Muslim Canadian community. The classic and most public example was that of Imam Delic, whom officials from a number of departments considered a valued interlocutor because he often participated in a variety of fora. However, given his association with the Canadian Islamic Congress, whose previous president Al-Masry had made unacceptable comments about attacks on Israelis, Delic was effectively placed on a "blacklist."[187] The government also appeared to prefer interlocutors from minority Muslim groups (Ahmadiyyas, Ismailis) or the more secular groups (Canadian Muslim Congress, Canadian Council of Muslim Women).

But for officials, who were trying to understand better the diversity and dynamics among Muslim Canadians, limiting discussion to a narrow range of Muslim Canadian groups was counterproductive. In the end, officials went ahead under the radar and initiated discussion with a range of Muslim Canadians and groups.[188]

While the debate over whether to limit the scope to violent radicalization or extremism was never resolved because of the overall direction of the Multiculturalism Program towards integration, the broader interpretation that included non-violent radicalization and social cohesion issues largely prevailed.

---

[185] Working draft, memo to the Minister, Update on Radicalization Work, winter 2011.

[186] Unfortunately not noted in the CCRS minutes of that meeting given its focus on Air India.November 12-14, 2010, Report of the Commission of Inquiry into the Bombing of Air India Flight 182.

[187] This became public when Defense Minister MacKay banned his appearance at a Ministry of National Defense Islamic History Month in October 2010. See MacKay bans imam's appearance at event for Islamic History Month, *The Globe and Mail*, updated 23 August 2012.

[188] One Montreal-area mosque visit, for example, provided some interesting insights into more conservative groups, as well as some of the limits and risks. While officials let pass a Palestinian poster showing all of Israel and the West Bank as Palestine during the first visit, officials did note the absence of women in the discussions.

POLICY ARROGANCE OR INNOCENT BIAS

Efforts to develop a coordinated, whole-of-government strategy culminated in 2012 with Building Resilience Against Terrorism: Canada's Counter-terrorism Strategy, issued by Public Safety. The *Prevent* element (cribbing the name from the UK) remained largely a security agency plan, rather than a whole-of-government strategy, but did note in passing that other departments, including CIC, "have supporting programs that directly or indirectly help mitigate the threat of violent extremism in Canada and abroad" by pursuing the following government-wide objectives:[189]

- Resilience of communities to violent extremism and radicalization is bolstered.

- Violent extremist ideology is effectively challenged by producing effective narratives to counter it.

- The risk of individuals succumbing to violent extremism and radicalization is reduced.[190]

While the role of the multiculturalism program in radicalization and extremism was comparatively minor in relation to the role of Public Safety and security agencies, all Western governments were grappling with understanding the root causes of radicalization. Some governments, such as the British government, were particularly ambitious, given the nature of these issues within the UK in the aftermath of the 7/7 bombings.

Within the Canadian context, the multiculturalism program provided a grants and contributions mechanism that allowed a number of small projects to proceed, something that Public Safety lacked at the time. It was useful in the range of interdepartmental and international discussions to have such examples to point to, and helped the program play more effectively in those fora.

Of course, the main focus had to be on police and intelligence work, due to the nature of the risks and threats (even amateur terror can be deadly). Ultimately, one of the prices one has to pay in a democratic society is a certain degree of risk that an individual, or group of individuals, will — for whatever misguided reason — take up violence. Just as we cannot eradicate crime, we cannot eradicate radicalization and extremism; we can only reduce the risk of serious incidents. This is another example where policy modesty, in terms of recognizing the limits of government and related interventions, can help ensure a more focused and realistic approach.

---

[189] The annex to the Strategy did mention the respective roles of departments. Much of CIC's role, naturally enough, focused on immigration and admissibility concerns, but some mention of the social policy role was made:

> CIC is also responsible for ensuring that newcomers and citizens participate to their full potential in fostering an integrated society. One of the key objectives of CIC's Multiculturalism Program is to build an integrated, socially cohesive society.

[190] Building Resilience Against Terrorism: Canada's Counter-terrorism Strategy, February 2012. The government also invested considerable resources in understanding the root causes of terrorism, including the establishment of The Kanishka Project in 2011. See Stephen Harper's search for the root causes of terrorism, *Macleans*, 20 April 2013.

The broader question of the risks related to non-violent extremism were harder to address. After all, it is no crime to think differently or to choose to live outside society in a democratic society. Nonetheless, from the perspective of integration and social cohesion, there are risks to society should larger numbers of people choose to exclude themselves from the broader community. Again, however, that is the price one pays for living in a democratic society.

Chapter 6

Machinery Change: 2008

From Canadian Heritage to CIC

Throughout this policy transformation, the government also implemented a parallel machinery change. In October 2008, responsibility for the multiculturalism program was shifted from Canadian Heritage to CIC, though under the mandate of the same Minister, Jason Kenney. The move diluted the expertise of multiculturalism officials, both in the broader government-wide context and within the new department.

How a cabinet is organized, and how responsibilities are assigned to particular departments, makes a big difference at both the political and bureaucratic levels. Having a separate minister, even a junior minister, provides a distinct seat at interdepartmental and other fora. Each department has its key priorities, or "centre of gravity" around which departmental resources, focus and culture are clustered.

The transfer of the multiculturalism program from PCH to CIC was no exception, and began a dilution of focus on multiculturalism issues, similar to what happened when citizenship was folded into CIC in 1994. Having one minister responsible for citizenship, immigration, and multiculturalism simplified policy coordination while reducing political-level attention to multiculturalism. Moreover, dispersing multiculturalism across CIC's functional model, the reality of CIC's "centre of gravity" or focus on immigrant selection, reallocation of resources, and the operational culture of CIC further reduced emphasis on long-term integration issues, facilitated implementation of desired policy changes, and greatly weakened the influence of the program in government.

CONTEXT

Before the formal machinery change of 30 October 2008, the Multiculturalism and Human Rights Branch at Canadian Heritage was a largely self-contained, integrated policy and program branch, with policy, research, and grants and contributions (G&C) operations, public education, and a variety of administrative services all under the Director General. The Branch reported to the Assistant Deputy Minister (ADM) of Citizenship and Heritage; other branches (e.g, Official Languages, Aboriginal Affairs) were similarly organized, also under the same ADM. This reflected the community orientation, the reality of working with different stakeholder groups, and the absence of providing services to individual Canadians at Canadian Heritage — although there were linkages made, both at the policy and operational levels, between multiculturalism, official language, and aboriginal issues. The last of these was buttressed with an overall conceptual framework, referred to at times as pluralism, capturing all the different elements of Canadian diversity and how they reflected a Canadian tradition of balance between accommodation and integration.

The Multiculturalism Program had a junior Minister, or Secretary of State (SoS), a position that provided a strong political focus to the activities of the Branch. In practice, there was a direct and continuous connection between the SoS and his office, demonstrated by an active policy and program renewal process (e.g., Chinese Head Tax program, Community and National Historical Recognition Programs, support to Secretary of State community outreach, new multiculturalism priorities) in the few years prior to the transfer to CIC.

While national headquarters was vertically integrated, regional staff typically handled multiple programs, particularly in the smaller offices.

The transfer to CIC, along with the normal challenges of fitting into a different department, also meant that there was a need for major reorganization given the different structural model of CIC. CIC had been organized on a functional basis since 2006, when the department underwent a major reorganization to separate out the policy and organizational functions. As a result, most non-policy functions were shifted to operational or functional areas to help strengthen the policy capacity and focus of the Department. This applied not only to programs that pertained to service and to individual applicants (e.g., immigration selection, citizenship proofs, and grants) — which has traditionally been the focus of CIC — but also to grants and contributions (e.g., settlement programming).

In contrast with the more project and community-building emphasis of the multiculturalism G&Cs (which included historical recognition), CIC's G&C programming primarily took the form of service contracts, with ongoing renewals, for the provision of employment preparedness or language training.

PROCESS AND ORGANIZATION

At the senior level, the ADM of Corporate Services from each department chaired transition teams for each department, and convened regular meetings of the two teams (CIC and PCH) to drive the process forward. I was in the uncomfortable position of having to provide advice and comments to both sides, in a manner that would allow me to leave Canadian Heritage and arrive at CIC with both departments relatively happy.

As it turned out, both sides were pragmatic. The financial and related resource discussions proceeded smoothly. Enough people at CIC remembered the difficult experience of severing CIC's enforcement functions and transferring them to Canada Border Services Agency (CBSA), so they were determined to avoid another similar experience. Canadian Heritage took a similar approach and within a few months an agreement was reached on how much funding to transfer:

$8.7 million for salaries, $5.9 million for operating, and $22.8 million for grants and contributions.[191]

The welcoming environment and collegiality of CIC also greatly facilitated the integration process. As part of both the change in management structure and the change in management process, a number of measures were taken:

- Weekly meetings the first few months, including regional staff plugged in by conference call, updating all staff on transition planning and issues. As integration proceeded, the frequency decreased and these were no longer necessary by April 2009;

- An all-staff meeting, with significant regional representation, in December 2009, with the Minister and CIC senior management explaining further the rationale and synergies between multiculturalism and the rest of CIC's mandate;

- Appropriate Ministerial and Deputy Ministerial messaging at critical moments of transition;

- Revision of CIC's Strategic Outcomes and Program Activity Architecture (PAA), in which the addition of Multiculturalism provided the critical mass for settlement, citizenship, foreign credential recognition, and multiculturalism to have an "integrated society" outcome, thus broadening CIC's mandate to long-term integration issues;

- Active participation by Multiculturalism in the various Medium-Term Planning processes to help CIC as a whole appreciate the impact of multiculturalism on the broad range of CIC programming;

- Development of integrated citizenship and multiculturalism story lines that respect the uniqueness of each but capture the policy shift towards more meaningful citizenship and more explicit integration aspects to multiculturalism, and how these reinforce one another;

- Inclusion of broader departmental aspects in each Citizenship and Multiculturalism all-staff retreat (e.g., panels with other Director Generals, Deputy Minister participation etc.); and

- Upon the transfer of National Headquarters (NHQ) Multi and Historical Recognition staff to Operations Sector and concomitant with the launch of the new Inter-Action Multi G&C program, a retreat involving all NHQ and regional Multi staff along with Historical Recognition staff was held in June 2010. The Minister attended two sessions, one to deliver a speech on what he has learned in his "practicum" in the communities, and a second session to respond to questions from staff.

At the operational level, officials needed to implement reorganization and transfer control to the appropriate functional leads within CIC, in order to implement a clear (or clearer) separation between the policy and program functions.

---

[191] From working CIC documents and 2009-10 Supplementary Estimates A. Includes both the Historical Recognition Program (sunsetted in 2012-13) and both national and regional multiculturalism staff. Actual amounts may have undergone minor further revision.

Moreover, it was necessary to find an organizational home for the multiculturalism function. The departure of the Director General for Citizenship provided an opportunity to merge the Citizenship and Multiculturalism branches early in 2009, on policy grounds (reinforcing linkages), operational consistency (ensuring, in the final outcome, comparable responsibilities and resources to other branches), and financial reasons (saving the cost of one DG and office). CIC later created a new position in 2010, Associate Assistant Deputy Minister (AADM) in the Policy Sector, the purpose of which was to provide greater focus, coordination, and oversight to the various policy areas responsible for integration: citizenship, foreign credential recognition, integration/settlement, and multiculturalism.

The following table captures the main groups and functions transferred, over time, to other functional groups within CIC, with the Policy Sector retaining the policy functions:

Table 12: Transition to CIC Organizational Structure[192]

Group	Transferred to:	FTEs	O&M
Public Education (awards and events)	Communications Branch	5	$750,000
Regional program staff (multi grants and contributions)	Regions	37.5	$149,640
Research Group	Research and Evaluation Branch	4	$14,275
National Program Staff (multiculturalism and historical recognition grants and Contributions)	Integrations Programs Management Branch (new)	27	$201,062

While the public education and regional program staff moved immediately upon transfer, the research staff moved later, in 2009. The national program staff was only transferred in 2010, given the need for CIC to create a dedicated operational group for grants and contributions headed by a Director General, to avoid getting buried under the Operational Management and Coordination Branch (OMC).[193]

Some transfers were smoother and more effective than others. In particular, the Public Education group continued to deliver existing programming more efficiently during the transfer, while creating new capacity to deliver citizenship-related public education. Other transitions were more challenging. For example, Canadian Heritage had portfolio leads: one regional Director General served as a co-lead with each policy lead (the Director General responsible for the

---

[192] FTEs: Full-Time Equivalents (or people), O&M: Operations and Maintenance Funds (as distinct from salaries and grants and contributions).

[193] OMC was responsible for all operational coordination in Canada and tended to focus on CIC's "centre of gravity" on operational issues related to immigration, with less attention paid to citizenship and integration issues.

particular program and policy) to improve national coherence and coordination across the regions. CIC did not divide responsibility in this manner. Dealing with each regional DG, rather than a single DG with a national coordination role, made the initial transition and integration harder than it needed to be.[194]

Interestingly, while the CIC functional model was strictly applied to the Multiculturalism Program, some anomalies remained within CIC at the time:

- **Citizenship Citation:** This annual award is delivered by Citizenship Program Delivery & Promotion, Operations Sector, rather than by the Communications Branch, responsible for all the multiculturalism and other departmental award programs. Similarly, the annual contribution to the Institute for Canadian Citizenship (ICC) is still managed by the Citizenship and Multiculturalism Branch, rather than by the Integration Programs Management Branch.

- **Foreign Credentials Recognition Office (FCRO) G&Cs and Federal Internship for Newcomers Program (FINP):** As FCRO was newer to CIC than Multiculturalism and still in transition in 2011, the G&C function had not yet been transferred to Operations at that time. The FINP remained within FCRO, within the Policy Sector, rather than the Operations Sector.

While the above changes, along with some administrative support services, reflected the shift to the CIC functional model, in winter 2011 most of the Multiculturalism Partnerships and Engagement Division was transferred to the International and Intergovernmental Relations Branch to develop and strengthen CIC's overall engagement capacity (11 FTEs and $40,000 in O&M). This reduced substantially the capacity of the Branch to manage the range of partnership and engagement activities, including the International Holocaust Awareness Alliance, antisemitism initiatives, Multiculturalism Annual Report and Champions, federal-provincial multiculturalism dialogue, the Global Centre for Pluralism and the Canadian Race Relations Foundation.[195]

IMPLICATIONS

The transition to CIC thus required a significant alignment of all non-policy functions to other sectors within CIC, consequently refocusing on the policy function for multiculturalism. At the

---

[194] The more substantive challenge, which varied from region to region given the difference between CIC regions in delivery (or lack thereof) of grants and contributions programs, was that even in regions that delivered grants and contributions programs, these were more service contracts for settlement services and language training, largely decided through a "call for proposal" (CFP) process rather than the community development work of multiculturalism program staff. This eventually became less important in 2010 when the multiculturalism program moved towards a CFP process as well, although the difference remained between community development orientation and settlement services.

[195] This was comical, as I was informed of the decision to transfer the entire division without any time for discussion of the implications. I was able to "claw back" five positions from the 15 initially being transferred to preserve some capacity. The receiving branch had not been consulted either and had no idea what to do with the people. In retrospect, I should have read the tea leaves more carefully.

political and senior bureaucratic level, the transfer of the Multiculturalism Program from Canadian Heritage to CIC in October 2008 had a number of implications:

- One Minister responsible for improving policy and program coherence in citizenship, immigration and multiculturalism, combined with the political function of outreach to ethnic and faith-based communities (this political function was subsequently separated in the Cabinet shuffle of July 2013);

- Without a dedicated Minister responsible for multiculturalism, the program was less visible to CIC itself, the government as a whole, and the public;

- No separate multiculturalism "voice" in interdepartmental or other domestic or international fora. The long-term integration perspective of multiculturalism has become lost in the newcomer and visitor "centre of gravity" of CIC priorities;[196]

- An early decision not to change the name of CIC to Citizenship, Immigration and Multiculturalism, given the optics and cost of a departmental name change;[197]

- Internally, within the bureaucracy, a less direct relationship between the Multiculturalism Program and the Minister, replaced by a bureaucratic version of the "great chain of being," and consequently heavier and slower bureaucratic processes and procedures; and,

- The luck of having a Minister with a strong interest in multiculturalism provided an additional incentive for CIC as a whole to consider the broader impact of multiculturalism on CIC. Ministers matter; otherwise normal departmental inertia sets in, in terms of focus on current activities and resources (multiculturalism is about 1 percent of CIC total Vote 5 G&C resources). This is not unique to multiculturalism: citizenship also enjoyed a higher profile given an active political agenda, which also contributed to reshaping CIC's emphasis.[198]

Throughout the transition and the transfer, some other implications for the bureaucracy and program were of note:

- While one can make a case for either the PCH (vertically integrated) or CIC (functionally integrated) organizational models, the case for the latter is more self-evident when it comes to providing services to individuals than it is for programs with a community focus. As noted

---

[196] On the other hand, the linkages between short-term and long-term integration challenges were strengthened and became more explicit within CIC.

[197] It is unclear whether this was the only reason or whether the overall political direction to downplay multiculturalism also played a part. There was some confusion in the first month of the transfer. The title of the Minister, however, included multiculturalism. When important to the government (i.e., the addition of the word "royal" to the various branches of the Canadian Forces), cost of new signs and business cards were not an issue.

[198] In contrast to central agencies constantly challenging ministerial initiatives when Minister Kenney was a junior Minister at Canadian Heritage, becoming a full Minister at CIC silenced many of the mixed signals officials had received about whether or not the Minister enjoyed the full confidence of PMO. His "promotion" helped settle that issue, and made for a more normal challenge function.

earlier, for CIC, where even settlement G&Cs are a means to providing employment and language services to individuals, this model is a valid approach. It does present more of a challenge for the community-based approach of multiculturalism, and may well over time weaken connections between policy and projects and related feedback mechanisms. Other departments do not make this separation from G&C policy and G&C operations, recognizing the importance of that link;

- At least up to mid-2011, CIC officials had not thought through the implications of the PAA Strategic Outcomes in terms of governance. CIC governance essentially replicates the organizational model (e.g., Business Operations Committee and Operations Management Committee for operations, Policy Committee for policy). While there is some cross membership, it may be warranted to consider models that would ensure a focus on strategic outcomes across operations and policy. There were some tentative steps under the Department's Strategic Outcome 3 (SO3 - *Newcomers and citizens participate to their full potential in fostering an integrated society*) in this direction;

- The importance of framework documents, such as the Program Activity Architecture (PAA), and processes, such as medium-term planning, are critical in any such transition. These processes helped CIC understand the implications of being responsible for Multiculturalism, in the sense of long-term integration issues, and similarly helped Multiculturalism understand the CIC environment.

- Change management is never-ending. Close to two years after the move to CIC, Multiculturalism staff were less satisfied than their Citizenship colleagues according to an internal version of the Public Service Employee Survey in June 2010.

While the decision to make a machinery change is the prerogative of the Prime Minister, implementation comes down to a series of decisions at both the political and bureaucratic levels. Smaller organizations have to fit into the overall structure and culture of the larger organization. No matter how welcoming and open an environment — and CIC was particularly welcoming — such a machinery change is akin to a takeover, with all the workplace cultural transitions that this entails.

One of the ironies of this machinery change was the degree to which it was welcomed by the Citizenship Program. Citizenship was outside of CIC's centre of gravity and had been under managed for years. The arrival of multiculturalism was welcomed as a way to provide more support, both rhetorically and substantially, to the citizenship program. The desired result was to have one stronger and better resourced Citizenship and Multiculturalism Branch.

As we have seen, however, the dispersal of the multiculturalism program across CIC's functional model, combined with resource reductions, and the latest decision to split the Ministerial political function (Minister Kenney) from the departmental function (Minister Alexander), has likely fatally weakened the multiculturalism program.

Chapter 7

So What Kind of "Yes Minister" Will That Be?

While this book has focused on the case study of the "reset" of citizenship and multiculturalism policy from the eyes of one official, many of the elements of the challenge to the public service are not unique, given the nature of many of the policy changes implemented by the Harper government.

On a personal level, looking back at this process of citizenship and multiculturalism policy and program renewal makes me realize just how fortunate I am to have lived through such a period. Nothing is more deadening or uninteresting than to be responsible for files that do not interest the Minister. That was not the case for me, and while some of my colleagues may disagree, working with a Minister (and Minister's Office) with a strong sense of purpose and direction makes for a more rewarding, if challenging, experience.

Yet from a broader perspective, the depth of the public service trauma precipitated by the philosophical reset in the government's citizenship and multiculturalism files is not to be underestimated. The lessons (for both elected officials and public servants) which can be drawn from this adventure are particularly useful when read as a case study in policy change management in general. There are any number of files across the federal bureaucracy where the current government has been willing to challenge long-entrenched assumptions and the policy *status quo*, a *status quo* inherited from many years of a more liberal and less assertive political tradition. Departments and agencies ranging from Statistics Canada to CIDA, DFAIT and Environment are areas where the dichotomy between "expert" officials and their democratically elected bosses were so strained that the capacity to collaborate broke down to the point where policy development and policy decision making were essentially relocated to the Ministers' offices or to even to the Prime Minister's Office itself.

The tension was further exacerbated by the challenge to public service expertise happening on two levels:

1. A fundamental challenge to evidence-based policy making and the basic capacity of government to have the needed information to support informed decision-making. Cancellation of the mandatory census, reduction of scientific expertise across government, and the weakening of some of the institutional mechanisms to provide independent advice have long-term consequences for future governments.

2. Less fundamental changes to individual policy areas, which can be reversed or strengthened by future governments if desired. The capacity of future governments is not constrained on the basis of fundamental capacity and knowledge, although all policy changes take time, are complex, and encounter stakeholder and other resistance.

Given that the Harper government operated on both of these levels, the impact of its decisions will be long-lasting. While officials may or may not agree with particular policy changes, they can more easily understand and accept individual policy shifts than the more fundamental reduction of the capacity of future governments to make future choices. More policy modesty on the part of the government in terms of capacity reductions is needed.

While the experts can be wrong, and, as I have argued, have limits to their knowledge and bias, their views on both narrow implementation and broader policy direction questions remain necessary. Their views are part of a designed informal "balance of power" to keep elected officials in check. When the relationship breaks down, perhaps because officials overstep their advisory role, and ministers and their staff are unwilling to even consider advice, the quality and usefulness of policy advice and implementation is weakened.

At this broader level, working with a government decidedly breaking with policy continuity poses a major challenge for public servants. Given the complexity of social policy issues, and thus the requirement for expert knowledge, advice, and expertise, such a challenge to the public service role starts off by being demoralizing and even traumatic. From the political level's perspective, being constantly challenged by "know-it-all" officials (who are sometimes ideologues in disguise), armed with extensive research and studies, the sophistication of *Yes Minister* techniques, and the general arrogance of the expert, is equally aggravating. The difference between the softer bureaucratic style, where ideology is implied rather than proclaimed, and the more blunt and direct expression of ideology by the political level, further exacerbates tension. However, falling into a pattern of rolling one's eyes at each other and viewing the political-bureaucratic relationship as antagonistic is not productive and does not lead anywhere. After all, governments are elected, whereas public servants are not, and governments are ultimately accountable for their decisions before the public.

All of us, including public servants, have our biases and prejudices, which influence our evidence base, networks, and advice. While the requirement under the *Code of Values and Ethics* to be non-partisan is relatively straightforward, the requirement to be impartial is less so, more of a Platonic ideal than reality, given our inherent cognitive biases. Getting over the non-recognition of our biases is a fundamental challenge. This does not mean abandoning our expertise, knowledge and experience, but rather being more conscious of their limits. Being fundamentally challenged — being forced to switch from System 1 to System 2 thinking, to use Kahneman's phrase — is helpful in improving the quality and range of advice. All public servants should read Kahneman to enhance their self-awareness, and reflect on the implications for policy and program advice. In a number of the issues outlined above, the new policy directions forced the bureaucracy to consider additional forms of evidence, rather than relying on the tried and true large-scale surveys and familiar research.

In this way, the reset also forced a degree of policy modesty. Public servants did not have the complete picture and were often too disconnected from the realities on the ground to understand the limitations of their analysis and advice. Finding one's way in this new relationship was a challenge: one had to accept a different perspective and find ways to work within it, while maintaining the integrity of the evidence-base and capacity for fearless — or at least frank — advice.[199]

Similarly, one needs to keep in mind the limits of public policy, and that many interventions are limited in impact. So much of citizenship and multiculturalism policy and practices happens through other levels of government and a wide range of public and private institutions. The federal government's role is limited; policy swings in one direction may have less dramatic results than anticipated, due to the inevitable complexities of a modern, diverse society like Canada's. Each of the case studies cited, important as they may have been in their own way, could have less of an impact on the Canadian fabric than anticipated.

Just as society changes slowly, change is hard at both the individual and group levels and takes time. Some public servants found it harder than others; some remained in the "denial" or "anger" stages, or, equally unhelpfully, accepted the shift so readily that they risked losing sight of their policy advisory role. Much of the denial and anger was perceived, not incorrectly, as disloyalty to the government, given the depth of the resistance.

While leadership and management are essential, the inertia and resistance to change in much of the public service complicates efforts to develop and implement new policies and programs. In the end, of course, the public service adapts, as it should and must. Future governments with different priorities will also face inertia should they wish to change direction, but this may be less challenging than the shift under the Conservative government. It is more likely that a subsequent government would pivot back to greater acceptance of public service expertise, social science, and other evidence.

With this specific but widely applicable experience in mind, a number of reflections on the potential issues with future policy shifts emerge.

Ideology, Evidence and Anecdote

Each of us, whether at the political or official levels, has an underlying ideology, perspective and bias. The question is whether or not we can acknowledge this, and in so doing, become more aware of the limits of our own perspectives and related evidence, and open to listening to alternative viewpoints. This is not to argue in favor of "truthiness," to use Stephen Colbert's phrase, for there are objective facts. But society is complex, and no complete and comprehensive picture exists. The facts we choose to make our arguments provide a partial view of society and the predicted effects of policy changes. Moreover, how we choose to interpret facts has an element of subjectivity that needs to be acknowledged by all parties in the policy-making process.

For a bureaucracy that prides itself on evidence-based policy, this may be particularly difficult as it means accepting that the evidence we respond to and accept may reflect confirmation and other biases. After all, officials who spend most of their career in economic or social policy are largely the product of the conventional perspectives of those fields. Combined with normal bureaucratic inertia and its inherent conservatism or prudence (there are risks to sticking one's

---

[199] Depending on the issue, this can cut both ways. Many within CIC welcomed the change in immigration policies to reduce perceived abuse and imbalance, and likely chafed under some of the policies and priorities of previous governments. From initial concern about Minister Kenney having too many priorities, the tide quickly shifted to: "we have an opportunity to get some of the changes we have long pressed for, let's not waste it …"

neck out!), and the smoothing out of policy differences in all intra- and interdepartmental fora, this influences government's tendency to reinforce existing positions.

The question is not whether to jettison evidence-based policy; existing economic and social policy remains valid and important in providing advice to Ministers. But officials need to acknowledge some of the weaknesses (e.g., lack of granularity) and it has to be more inclusive and accept anecdotes, particularly when backed by extensive Ministerial outreach, as a valid complement to what the macro trends indicate. Anecdotes can and do lead to bad policy (e.g., the "tough on crime" policies, the canceling of the mandatory long form census) but they are part of the political reality. In the case of citizenship, anecdotes were important in highlighting long-neglected citizenship program integrity issues; in the case of multiculturalism, anecdotes were important in broadening the program focus beyond mainstream/minority relations to those between and among all communities.

Program versus political risk

Officials focus on program risk, whether these risks are legal, policy, administrative or operational, and rightly so. In providing advice to the political level, officials are generally better at identifying potential risks than they are at identifying the probability of these risks occurring. Again, officials, while not "crying wolf," will tend to stress potential downside risks, often as a necessary counterweight to ministerial direction on policy and programs, where the focus on "getting it done" may downplay risks.

Officials tend toward the theoretical; politicians tend toward the practical. The political level tends to be more concerned about the probability of a risk actually occurring, especially, but not exclusively, in the context of the electoral calendar. For example, in the case of the historical recognition program, officials were able to identify the potential risks of treating different communities differently, but were less able to understand how the Minister and his staff would manage the political risks and, in so doing, minimize the program risk.

Officials need to get better at separating out potential and probable risks, be more sensitive to the different calculations of program and political risks, and find ways, in their presentation of potential and probable risks, to provide clearer yet attuned advice to ministers. In the end, of course, the Minister will have a different risk calculation than officials, but how it is framed in departmental advice can make any decision more aware and informed.

Balance process with delivery

Ministers will take shortcuts when available, particularly in a context where the overall government direction is towards streamlined decision-making and reduced public debate and oversight. Ministers have a limited time to implement policy changes before a change in portfolio or government, whereas officials have a long-term perspective on risk, as many of them will still be around to deal with consequences, foreseen or unforeseen, of policy changes. Tight timelines are an inevitable result, with all the necessary compromises these entail.

While from a public policy and democratic perspective due process is essential for the long-term sustainability of policy and program changes, officials are largely powerless to impose good process unless required by regulation or legislation. The contrast between the accelerated process to develop *Discover Canada* and the related citizenship test (i.e., the absence of focus group testing), and the more measured approach of changes in language requirements illustrates this.

Nevertheless, within this context officials need to find ways to "impose" a certain minimum process to minimize risks to Canadians, and build in safety mechanisms to accompany excessively hasty policy and program changes, including building in some safety mechanisms. For instance, in the case of the new citizenship test, detailed question-by-question results, along with a second chance to write the test during the implementation phase, while not ideal, alleviated some of the potential program (and political) impact of the significant failure rates during the first few months.

The key may be developing, to the extent possible, early feedback mechanisms to signal issues and allow for recommended corrective action. Additional feedback may come from affected groups, the media, and opposition parties.[200] The more the impact of the policy and program changes is felt in the short run, the more effective the feedback. However, any work (beyond media lines!) to allow for an upfront built-in process of adjustment may help the government deal with any public pressure should the government so wish. Of course, in the long-term (through subsequent government mandates), the regular cycle of government-required evaluations will provide after-the-fact assessment and feedback.

Maintain independent capacity

All governments have their priorities, and the public service has to ensure that it delivers on these priorities. Yet some issues, or approaches to issues, may be overlooked, whether consciously or unconsciously. Maintaining policy capacity to increase understanding of issues that may not be "the flavour of the day" remains a challenge, one exacerbated during a time of tight resources. The Harper government has made significant cuts in such core policy capacity with long-term impact. Given this government-wide approach, there are limits to what senior executives can achieve in their resource, staffing, and time-allocation decisions.[201]

Machinery matters

Cabinet and government machinery make a big difference to the visibility and importance of programs. This happens at a number of levels:

1. Ministerial: Having a distinct minister responsible for Multiculturalism, when the program was housed at Canadian Heritage, meant the program had more public visibility. After all, a minister has to serve, make speeches, find issues, set direction, and increase his or her public profile. Just as citizenship's profile under the Secretary of State for Canada gradually diminished when it was folded into CIC in 1994 (the immigration 'centre of gravity'), the same long-term trend is happening with respect to

---

[200] Or not. No groups complained about the high refusal rates by Minister Kenney under the multiculturalism G&C program.

[201] CIC, in meeting the high demands of policy and program renewal in immigration, essentially merged its strategic policy unit and immigration levels policy, staffing it with a highly experienced executive in immigration matters, with the inevitable result of further strengthening CIC's "centre of gravity" and weakening long-term strategic thinking. Given that "in the long run, we're dead," and given the reality of the demanding policy agenda, this was understandable, but not without implications.

multiculturalism. While an exceptional Minister like Jason Kenney can have an active program of policy renewal across his portfolio, this is the exception not the norm.[202]

2. Interdepartmental: A separate Minister means a separate seat at the table at interdepartmental meetings on key horizontal files, as well as in external files. Rather than being filtered through the main CIC priorities of immigration and admissibility issues, long-term citizenship and multiculturalism issues have less of a distinct voice. For example, an integrated CIC position in interdepartmental discussion of security issues will focus on short-term admissibility and immigrant selection issues; when multiculturalism was at PCH, long-term integration and social cohesion issues would come to the fore.

3. Departmental structure and culture: A functional model like CIC has advantages in creating greater clarity between the policy and operational functions, but tends to reinforce the centre of gravity and allocate resources accordingly. A business line model like PCH provides more focused policy and program integration at the business line or program level, but increases rigidity and coordination issues between business lines. While the PAA structure acts as a counterweight, over time the centre of gravity will dominate. Arguably, for integration, citizenship and multiculturalism, the lines between pure policy and pure operations (e.g., citizenship ceremony design, G&C management) are less clear than for admissibility and immigration selection. Additionally, one of the legacies of the Cullen-Couture agreement transferring immigration selection and integration funding to Quebec meant CIC was largely uninterested in using the levers in citizenship and multiculturalism to highlight federal presence in Quebec.[203] A sharp contrast to PCH which had, and viewed itself as having, a strong role in Quebec.

In many ways, the collective impact for multiculturalism will, over time, become closer to the original Reform Party objective of 1996-97 of abolishing multiculturalism and strengthening a strong, common narrative of citizenship. The Cabinet shuffle of July 2013 and the separation of the political function, which remained under Minister Kenney, from the departmental function, under Minister Alexander, is significant in that context.[204] While political, community-based outreach is central to electoral strategies (the "fourth sister"), as evidenced by Minister Kenney's ongoing responsibility for this critical outreach, the substantive policy and program focus on long-term integration issues will continue to decline. This is a legitimate policy choice but it is striking just how little debate this change has provoked.

---

[202] One colleague with long experience in government noted that Minister Kenney was "'like Halley's comet, only coming by once every 76 years."

[203] An example of this was the preference for large citizenship ceremonies in Montreal on efficiency grounds, rather than focusing on how to increase the profile and meaningfulness of Canadian citizenship in Quebec. Another example, already mentioned, was refusal at the official level of a number of Quebec multiculturalism projects that would play a similar federal presence role.

[204] Jason Kenney to maintain hold on ethnic file despite move to jobs portfolio, *The Canadian Press*, 17 July 2013.

So What Kind of "Yes Minister" Will That Be?

In all of this, the challenge of "fearless advice and loyal implementation" remains, choosing when and where to be fearless, and how to pick one's battles. Knowing when one's advice may be influenced by one's own ideological biases ensures that when one picks one's battles, one does so from as objective a viewpoint as possible. Ideology, after all, is insidious and pervasive, a coherent framework of confirmation bias, and finding ways to become somewhat inoculated against these biases, or at least aware of them, is key.

Given this challenge, finding the balance between fearless advice (which can involve being perceived as unhelpful or disloyal), and implementation, or "getting it done," will always be difficult. In the early days of a new government or minister, the bias, conscious or not, may be more towards listing all the reasons why a proposed policy direction may be unduly risky; over time, something akin to the Stockholm syndrome may develop, where the policy directions of the government become increasingly internalized by the bureaucracy, leading to less rigorous advice. At the beginning of a new mandate, officials should be particularly conscious of the risk of appearing disloyal; later on, officials need to be aware of the even greater risk of losing their independent perspective. Both are problematic; the important thing is for officials to be aware and conscious of these risks and act accordingly.

In many ways, it is only when the advice of the public service emerges publicly through access to information and the media that the service's professionalism can be appropriately judged. The *Globe and Mail* and *Le Devoir* remain the litmus test; should an email, briefing note, or deck become public, would an informed reader conclude that the public service had done its job of serving the government of the day by providing quality advice?[205]

No one has a perfect record here, given the delicate balance between advice and implementation; while it is easier to judge in retrospect (hindsight is always 20/20), the task is harder in real time as public servants grapple with framing advice in a manner that will be considered, and not seen as obstructionist. All public servants can do is be more aware of their own thought processes, cognitive biases, and compromises, ensure that advice is documented and reads clearly to an outside observer, and, in the process, practice both professionalism and policy modesty.

---

[205] Waking up one Labour Day and seeing my name and one of my decks on radicalization on the front page of the *Globe and Mail* reminded me forcefully of this test: Heritage department takes aim at religious radicals, 1 September 2008. A less-flattering example can be found here. Support the minister, *Macleans*, 28 November 2011.

Acknowledgements

I would like to thank, first and foremost, Gilles Paquet and Robin Higham of the University of Ottawa for having encouraged me to write this account. They have been generous with their time and advice in helping me think through the story and issues related to the resetting of citizenship and multiculturalism. This book could not have been written without their ability to engage fearlessly, challenge relentlessly, and get me out of my comfort zone.

I have benefited from the experience, professionalism, judgement, and common sense of many public servant colleagues throughout my career, which has helped me find my own (admittedly imperfect) balance between "fearless advice and loyal implementation." Given the nature of government work, it was not possible to run draft sections by current public servants. I would like, however, to thank members of my former teams on citizenship and multiculturalism issues, who helped broaden my understanding and supported me. In addition, the section on historical recognition benefited from the knowledge of Sandy MacDonald and Tom Vigeant, but, of course, responsibility for the final text remains with me.

Thanks as well to my son, Alex Griffith, my editor, who, in addition to copy editing, made many additional and helpful substantive comments. Madeleine Levac lent her diligent eye to the final copy editing. My brother, Lorne Griffith, was incredibly patient with me in designing a cover that captured the key messages and approach of the book, as well as advising me on a number of design issues.

I would also like to thank my medical team at the Ottawa Hospital who supported me throughout my cancer journey, allowing me the time to complete this book.

Lastly, to Nazanine and both Alex and Roxanne, for their ongoing love and encouragement.

APPENDIX A: SOURCE COUNTRY OF IMMIGRANTS 2005 - 2012

Country	2005		2012		
	Number	Percent	Number	Percent	Change
China, People's Republic of	42,292	16.1%	33,018	12.6%	-3.5%
Philippines	17,525	6.7%	32,747	12.5%	5.8%
India	33,141	12.6%	28,943	11.0%	-1.6%
Pakistan	13,575	5.2%	9,931	3.8%	-1.4%
United States	9,263	3.5%	9,414	3.6%	0.1%
France	5,430	2.1%	8,138	3.1%	1.0%
Iran	5,502	2.1%	6,463	2.5%	0.4%
United Kingdom	5,864	2.2%	6,365	2.4%	0.2%
Haiti	1,719	0.7%	5,599	2.1%	1.5%
Korea, Republic of	5,819	2.2%	5,308	2.0%	-0.2%
Top Ten	**140,130**	**53.4%**	**145,926**	**55.6%**	**2.2%**
All Other Source Countries	122,112	46.6%	116,316	44.4%	-2.2%
Total	262,242	100.0%	262,242	100.0%	0.0%

Source: CIC Annual Immigration Reports, Facts and figures 2012: Immigration overview, Permanent Residents by Source Countries. Appendix G shows how this translates into source countries for new Canadian citizens.

APPENDIX B: CATEGORIES OF IMMIGRANTS 2005 - 2012

Immigrant Category (Entries)	2005		2012		Change 2012-2005
	Number	Percent	Number	Percent	
Total Economic class	156,313	34.6%	160,819	27.9%	-6.7%
Total Family class	63,373	14.0%	65,008	11.3%	-2.7%
Total Protected Persons (refugees)	35,775	7.9%	23,094	4.0%	-3.9%
Total Other	6781	1.5%	8966	1.6%	0.1%
Total Permanent Residents	**262,242**	**58.0%**	**257,887**	**44.8%**	**-13.3%**
Temporary Foreign Workers	122,365	27.1%	213,573	37.1%	10.0%
International Students	67,406	14.9%	104,810	18.2%	3.3%
Total Temporary Residents	**189,771**	**42.0%**	**318,383**	**55.2%**	**13.3%**
Total Permanent and Temporary Residents	**452,013**	**100.0%**	**576,270**	**100.0%**	

Changes in Immigrant Categories 2012-05

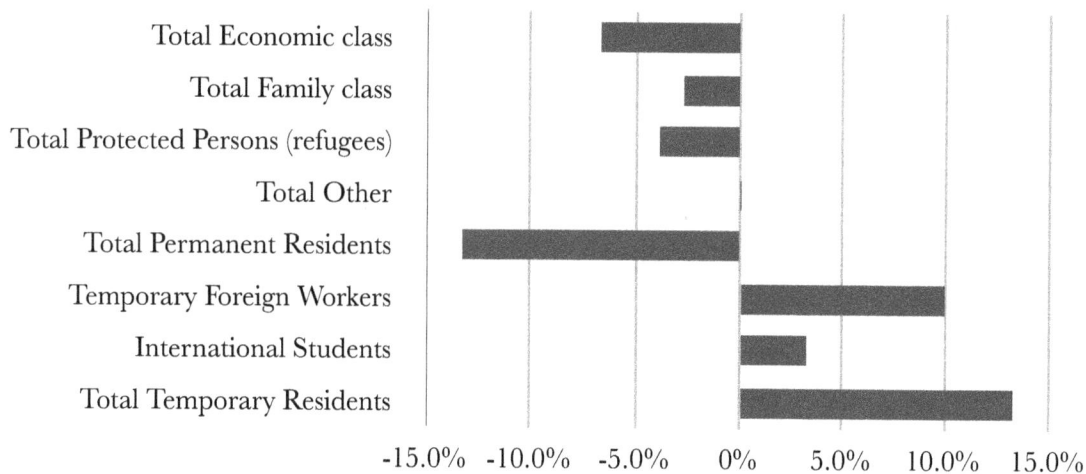

Source: CIC Annual Immigration Reports, <u>Facts and figures 2012: Immigration overview</u>, Permanent and temporary residents. Some simplification of the detailed CIC statistics for readability purposes. The graph shows permanent residents being largely flat, with the growth in temporary residents.

APPENDIX C: MINISTERIAL SPEECHES AND STATEMENTS BY COMMUNITY 2007 - 11

Community	2007	2008	2009	2010	2011	Total
General	23	6	5	6	9	49
Jewish	3	4	11	7	12	37
Chinese Canadian	17	7	0	4	2	30
Indo-Canadian	6	3	4	5	4	22
Black Canadian	7	2	1	2	2	14
Christian	2	3	3	3	3	14
Muslim	3	0	3	3	2	11
Asian Canadian	4	4	1	0	1	10
Ukrainian Canadian	1	4	0	3	2	10
Armenian Canadian	2	2	1	1	1	7
Muslim (Ismaili)	1	1	2	1	2	7
Polish Canadian	1	3	0	1	1	6
Greek Canadian	2	0	1	1	1	5
Vietnamese Canadian	0	1	1	1	2	5
Korean Canadian	0	2	0	1	1	4
Lebanese Canadian (Christian)	0	3	0	0	1	4
Philippine Canadian	0	1	1	1	1	4
Tibetan Canadian	0	2	1	0	1	4
Iranian Canadian	0	0	1	1	1	3
Jamaican Canadian	0	0	1	1	1	3
Muslim (Ahmadiyya)	1	2	0	0	0	3
Pakistani Canadian	0	1	0	0	2	3
Somali Canadian	0	2	1	0	0	3
South Asian Canadian	0	2	0	0	1	3
Buddhist	0	0	1	1	0	2
Macedonian Canadian	1	0	1	0	0	2
Arab Israeli Canadian	1	0	0	0	0	1
Baltic Canadian	0	1	0	0	0	1
Croatian Canadian	1	0	0	0	0	1
Czech Canadian	0	1	0	0	0	1
Italian Canadian	0	1	0	0	0	1
Iraqi Canadian (Christian)	0	0	0	0	1	1
Irish Canadian	0	0	0	0	1	1
Sudanese Canadian	1	0	0	0	0	1
Total	**77**	**58**	**40**	**43**	**55**	**273**

Source: Created from CIC website list of statements, speeches etc.

APPENDIX D: LAPSES IN MULTICULTURALISM PROGRAM G&CS

Fiscal Year	Year-End Authorities	Actual Spending	Spending as Percentage of Year-end Authorities
1999-00	$12,923,856	$12,913,787	99.9%
2000-01	$7,381,921	$6,525,141	88.4%
2001-02	$7,551,768	$7,451,281	98.7%
2002-03	$7,201,500	$7,200,158	100.0%
2003-04	$11,291,755	$11,208,955	99.3%
2004-05	$12,413,047	$12,356,212	99.5%
2005-06	$10,771,573	$10,492,122	97.4%
2006-07	$10,111,061	$9,255,864	91.5%
2007-08	$8,226,701	$7,121,785	86.6%
2008-09	$11,053,368	$4,147,619	37.5%
2009-10	$11,667,999	$4,205,565	36.0%
2010-11	$10,890,766	$6,829,468	62.7%

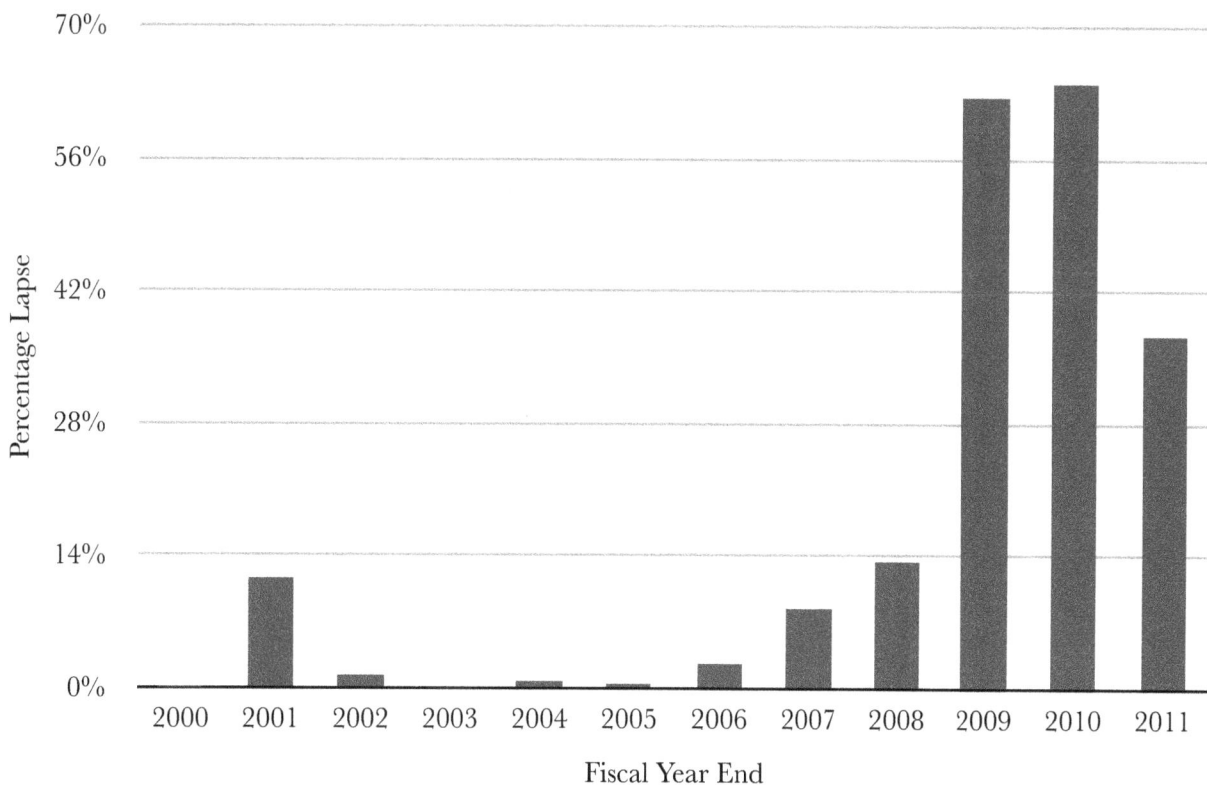

Source: Data taken from table in Question Period House Card, Multiculturalism Program Storyline, 27 January 2011, with 2010-11 data supplemented by CIC Main Estimates and Evaluations of the

Multiculturalism Program and Canada's Action Plan Against Racism (CAPAR). This only refers to core multiculturalism program G&C funding; as part of CAPAR, additional funds were appropriated for multiculturalism G&Cs (enhancement funding of around $5 million, if memory serves me correctly). As it happened, program spending never used any of these 'enhancement' funds which were reallocated, largely to meet Canadian Heritage expenditure reduction commitments. Current G&C funding for multiculturalism is $8.6 million (Reports on Plans and Priorities for 2012–2013).

Given that a number of earlier approved projects involved multi-year funding, the impact of the high refusal rates starting in 2007 and continuing on through 2009 only started to impact expenditures in the fiscal year 2008-09. There was a similar lag following the announcement of the new multiculturalism G&C program, Inter-Action, in June 2010.

APPENDIX E: KEY MINISTERIAL MESSAGES IN ANNUAL REPORTS OF THE CANADIAN MULTICULTURALISM ACT

Year	Key Messages
2003-4 PCH Liberal Government	Minister Chan • Embracing and managing diversity a distinguishing characteristic • Combat discrimination, promote cross-cultural understanding, and make Canadian institutions more representative • Contribute to the continuing evolution of our country • Data collection and research programs • More inclusive society • Charter of Rights and Freedoms • Equality of opportunity • Diversity source of strength and innovation • Economy, culture, and society benefit when Canadians of diverse backgrounds share talents, perspectives, and experience • Way of life … value at the heart of our collective identity • Belief that diversity is synonymous with success, prosperity and the future
2004-5 PCH New Conservative Government	Minister Oda • Promote inclusion and respect for diversity • Build a stronger, more cohesive, and more inclusive Canada • Strong sense of citizenship built on the commitment and contribution of all its citizens • Values and principles embodied in the Canadian Multiculturalism Act are respected • Multiculturalism … It is a source of our strength

PolicyArrogance or Innocent Bias

Year	Key Messages
2005-6 PCH (Canadian Heritage)	Minister Oda • Openness, cross-cultural understanding and mutual respect • Chinese Canadian Head Tax Program launched • Truly representative public service and an inclusive society Secretary of State Kenney • Outreach to all Canadians • Pluralistic society where language, religion, ethnic origins or race are not obstacles to fully participating in community life • Committed to ensuring that all citizens can take full part in our country's political, economic and cultural life • Model of both openness and cohesion in this world with its expanding exchanges between cultures • Modern programs and policies that are suited to today's reality • Respect their cultural roots while being an integral part of Canadian society • One of the most diverse, harmonious and creative societies of the 21st century
2006-7 PCH	Secretary of State Kenney • Shared values of democracy, freedom, human rights, and the rule of law • Leader among countries that embrace diversity • Canada as the home for the new Global Centre for Pluralism • "Pluralism allows individuals to retain their cultural, linguistic and religious heritage within a framework of shared citizenship." (PM quote) • Economic, social, and cultural integration • Promote integration in order to encourage prosperity and social cohesion
2007-8 CIC Transfer to CIC	Minister Kenney • Remembrance Day and honouring past • Citizenship oath to the Crown and meaning • Successful model of multiculturalism and pluralism • Constitutional framework for Aboriginal rights, minority language rights, and religious freedom • Invite new Canadians "to write the next chapter" of the Canadian story • Move of multiculturalism to CIC to "further inclusion, participation and shared citizenship for all Canadians"

Year	Key Messages

2008-9	Minister Kenney
	• *Discover Canada* includes a stronger, broader focus on Canada' values, history, and symbols, including our core values of freedom, democracy, human rights, and the rule of law
	• Unity-in-diversity approach to multiculturalism
	• Three new policy objectives:
	  • an integrated socially cohesive society;
	  • making institutions more responsive to the needs of Canada's diverse population; and,
	  • engaging in international discussions on multiculturalism and diversity
	• Membership in International Task Force on Holocaust Education, Remembrance and Research (now International Holocaust Remembrance Alliance)
	• Paul Yuzyk Award
	• Somali-Jewish Canadian Mentorship Project

2009-10	Minister Kenney • Build an integrated society that focuses on unity in our diversity • *Inter-Action* G&Cs launched: projects and new events stream (fairs and festivals) • *Discover Canada*, by placing increased emphasis on Canada's values, history and symbols, will promote civic memory and pride among newcomers and citizens alike. • Combat antisemitism together with all forms of racism and xenophobia • Canada will remain a country where people of all backgrounds and cultures can succeed and contribute to our collective future
2010-11	Minister Kenney • Intercultural and interfaith understanding, shared liberal values and the promotion of enhanced civic pride, and institutional responsiveness to the needs of a pluralistic society • *Discover Canada* updated to further strengthen its content on core Canadian values such as freedom, democracy, human rights, the rule of law and the equality of men and women (latter addition) • Launch of a new, online black history museum • Community Historical Recognition Program: acknowledge the mistakes in our past so that we can ensure that those mistakes are never repeated • Pluralism, intercultural understanding and equality of opportunity • Combat antisemitism through International Holocaust Remembrance Alliance • Encourage the members of all communities to participate fully in Canadian society, and to promote integration, pluralism, and civic engagement

Year	Key Messages
2011-12	Minister Kenney • Participation of all Canadians, not just newcomers • Deepen understanding of the values, history, institutions, rights, and responsibilities that unite us as Canadians • Intercultural and interfaith understanding, shared values, civic pride, and our commitment to a peacefully pluralistic society • Inter-Action and Community Historical Recognition • Black History Month and role in War of 1812 • Upcoming International Holocaust Remembrance Alliance Canadian Chairmanship • Engage governmental and community partners

Source: Summarized from PCH and CIC Annual Multiculturalism Reports

APPENDIX F: CITIZENSHIP OPERATIONAL STATISTICS AND BACKLOG

Citizenship Grants to New Canadians						
	2007	2008	2009	2010	2011	2012
Applications Received (Est.)	227,520	242,400	232,960	208,800	223,040	317,440
New Canadian Citizens	199,866	176,567	156,342	143,595	181,288	113,111
Increase in inventory (backlog)	27,654	65,833	76,618	65,205	41,752	204,329
Ceremonies Completed	2,802	2,011	1,957	1,743	1,944	1,664
Average New Citizens per Ceremony	71	88	80	82	93	68

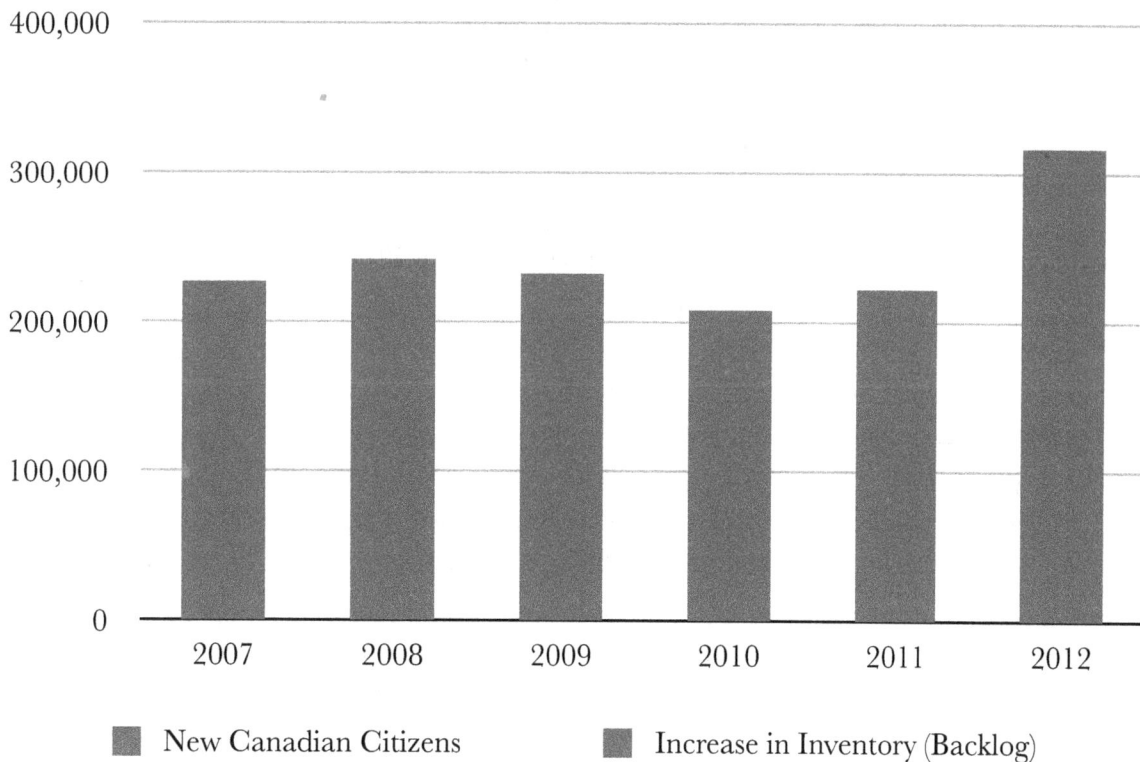

New Canadian Citizens   Increase in Inventory (Backlog)

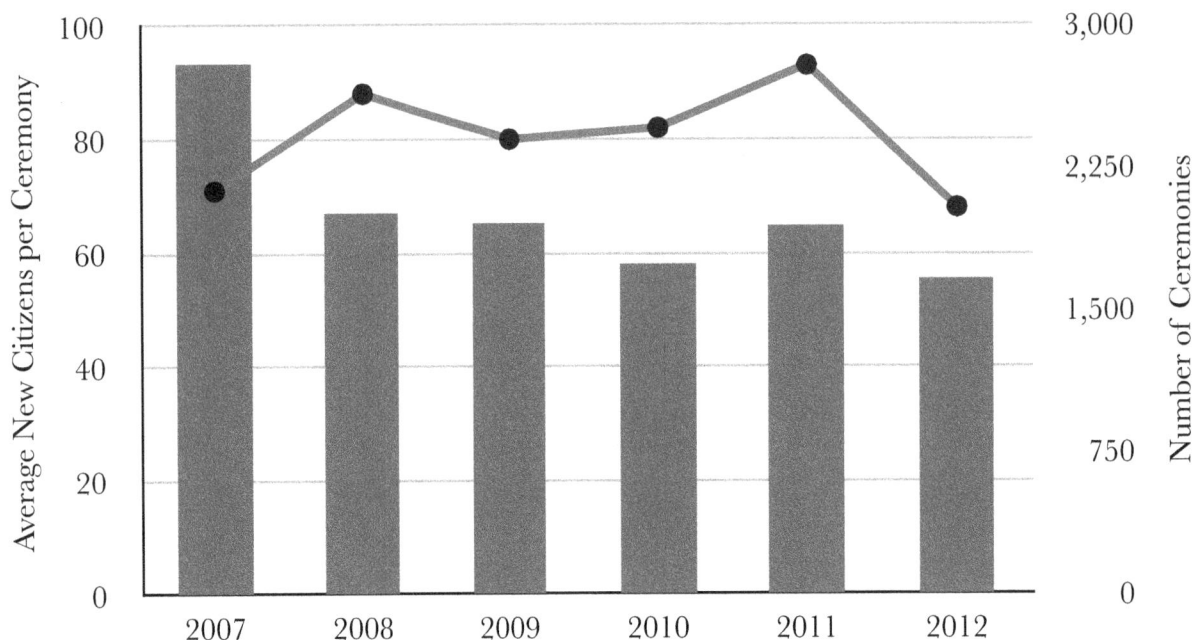

Source: CIC Operational Databases, 4th Quarter 2012. It is unclear what caused the jump in citizenship applications (from 223,000 to 317,000) in 2012, but clearly processing capacity also fell dramatically, from 181,000 to 113,000, or by 37 percent. Press accounts blame this for the increased fraud prevention measures, particularly residency determination, confirmed in the analysis in CIC Citizenship Management Quarterly Report, Second Quarter, FY 2012-13 (Operational Bulletin 407). $44 million was provided in Budget 2013 over two years to help address the backlog. See Citizenship application process blamed for growing wait list, CBC, 23 April 2013 and Immigration, Citizenship In Canada Budget 2013: Cost of Becoming a Canadian Set to Rise, Huffington Post, 21 March 2013.

Subsequent press accounts, based on ATIP release of internal CIC detailed operational management reports, also indicate that the introduction of new test questions and versions are another significant contributing factor. See More people failing revamped citizenship tests, CBC, 15 June 2013, based on the CIC Citizenship Management Quarterly Report, Second Quarter, FY 2012-13.

An additional factor may be the reductions in CIC's regional network implemented in 2012 as part of the Department's Strategic Review targets. 19 offices were closed. CIC Operational Bulletin 431 - In-Canada Office Closures and the Elimination of Front Counter Service, 1 June 2012.

Current processing times for Canadian citizenship are 25 months for routine applications, 35 for non-routine ones (Canadian citizenship, CIC website, June 2013). By comparison, Australia has a service standard of 60 calendar days, meeting this standard about 60 percent of the time (Citizenship program quarterly reports, Australia Department of Immigration and Citizenship website, quarterly report ending December 2012).

APPENDIX G: SOURCE COUNTRY OF NEW CANADIAN CITIZENS

Country of Birth	2007	2008	2009	2010	2011	Pass Rate	2012
India	25,793	20,834	17,400	18,964	22,217	80.2%	13,471
Philippines	12,197	11,667	11,068	11,607	16,153	85.3%	10,550
China (PRC)	24,348	21,026	16,011	13,417	15,565	89.2%	10,410
Pakistan	11,624	9,430	7,841	8,062	9,931	85.2%	5,630
USA	4,267	4,133	3,735	3,712	5,088	N/A	3,830
Iran	5,336	4,988	3,828	3,577	4,939	87.3%	3,527
England	3,936	3,624	3,323	3,494	4,705	N/A	3,448
South Korea	5,861	5,251	3,838	3,159	4,093	93.6%	3,071
Colombia	3,784	4,671	4,289	3,811	4,077	90.2%	2,541
Sri Lanka	4,703	3,692	3,187	2,915	3,347	67.2%	2,008
Total Top 10	**101,849**	**89,316**	**74,520**	**72,718**	**90,115**	**N/A**	**58,486**
Other	98,017	87,251	81,822	70,877	91,173	N/A	54,625
Total	**199,866**	**176,567**	**156,342**	**143,595**	**181,288**	**83.1%**	**113,111**

The major change is the increase of the proportion of new Philipino Canadians, matched by the decrease of new Chinese Canadians. As noted in Appendix F, there was a dramatic drop in new citizens in 2012.

As the country's mix of new citizens changed in 2012, the USA and England fell off the top 10 list. CIC does not post the complete statistics.

Source: CIC Operational Databases, 4th Quarter 2012.

Pass rate refers to the average for the March - December 2011 period, before changes were made in the test questions and versions in 2012. As CIC Citizenship Management Quarterly Report, Second Quarter, FY 2012-13, is a custom report using different timeframes, the top 10 countries are slightly different, with Vietnam (average pass rate of 67.7%) and Algeria (average pass rate of 88.2%) replacing the USA and England.

APPENDIX H: CIC DATASETS SORTED BY PROGRAM AREA

Name of Report (Adjusted)
CIC Operational Network At A Glance
Citizenship - Operational Statistics
Citizenship - Top 10 Source Countries - New Canadian Citizens (in Persons)
Foreign Workers - Total Entries Of Foreign Workers By Gender And Occupational Skill Level
Foreign Workers - Total Entries Of Foreign Workers By Province Or Territory And Urban Area
Humanitarian - Top 10 Source Countries - Refugee Claims At All Offices (in Persons)
Humanitarian - Total Entries Of Humanitarian Population By Gender And Age
Humanitarian - Total Entries Of Humanitarian Population By Province Or Territory And Urban Area
Humanitarian - Total Entries Of Humanitarian Population By Source Country
Permanent And Temporary Residents
Permanent Resident - Inventory
Permanent Resident - Inventory - Permanent Resident Card (in Persons)
Permanent Residents - Applicants Awaiting A Decision
Permanent Residents - Applications Processed Abroad And Processing Times
Permanent Residents - Applications Received At Case Processing Region (CPC-PRC) - Permanent Resident Card (in Persons)
Permanent Residents - Applications Received For Permanent Residents (in Persons)
Permanent Residents - Authorizations And Visas Issued For Permanent Residents (in Persons)
Permanent Residents - By Category
Permanent Residents - By Province Or Territory And Urban Area
Permanent Residents - By Source Country
Permanent Residents - Cards Produced By Canadian Bank Note (CBN)
Permanent Residents - Province Territory Of Declared Destination - Authorizations And Visas Issued For Permanent Residents (in Persons)
Permanent Residents - Summary By Mission
Permanent Residents - Top 10 Source Countries - Authorizations And Visas Issued For Permanent Residents (in Persons)
Permanent Residents - Visa Applications Received Abroad
Temporary Residents - Applications Processed Abroad And Processing Times
Temporary Residents - Applications Received For Temporary Residents (in Persons)
Temporary Residents - Point of Service - Applications Received for Temporary Residents (in Persons)
Temporary Residents - Top 10 Source Countries - Applications Received for Temporary Residents (in Persons)
Temporary Residents - Top 10 Source Countries - Visas, Permits and Extensions Issued for Temporary Residents (in Persons)
Temporary Residents - Visas, Permits and Extensions Issued for Temporary Residents (in Persons)

Source: Government of Canada Open Data website, <u>CIC Datasets</u>. The names of the datasets have been modified to ensure a consistent approach across the datasets, remove superfluous wording (e.g., Canada, English version), and allow for sorting by program.

www.ingramcontent.com/pod-product-compliance
Lightning Source LLC
Chambersburg PA
CBHW081657270326
41933CB00017B/3199